Acknowledgments

I dedicate this book to my beloved parents, my sister FZ and my wife who always believed in me. I could not have written this book without your immense support and patience

I also would like to thank my dear friends Idir, Nabil and David for their support.

Hicham KADIRI.

Who should read this book

This Book targets a large audience:

- IT Director
- Infrastructure Architect
- Infrastructure Consultant
- Technical Project Manager
- System /Network Engineer
- System/ Network Administrator
- Technical Support Engineer
- Anyone seeking knowledge about the design, deployment and management of Remote Desktop Services 2012 R2 infrastructure in a large environment.

Assumptions

There are no specific skills required overall for this book, but we expect that you have at least a minimal understanding of the following:

- Management and administration of Windows Server 2008 R2, 2012 or 2012 R2
- Management and administration of Terminal Server 2000/2003 or RDS 2008 /2008 R2
- Basic knowledges on Apps Publishing Solutions (e.g : Citrix XenApp or VMware View)
- TCP/IP Protocol
- Group Policy Object (GPO)
- Virtualized environments and Virtual Machines (VMs).

Software requirements

For many of the examples in this book, you will need the following softwares and OS images:

- Windows Server 2012 R2
- Windows 8.1
- SQL Server Express Edition 2012 & SMSSE
- SQL Server Native Client 2012
- Microsoft Office 2013 Pro Plus
- Notepad++ v6.8.1
- RDS Diagnostic Tool

Typography

The following typography is used in this book

 Tips or Recommendation

 Warning or Important Note

Using Code Examples

This book is here to help you get your job done. In general, you may use the code in this book in your programs, technical documentations and Blog. You do not need to contact the author for permission.

Therefore, you are invited to mention the source (book's name, author's name and publication date) if several parts of this book are copied on others supports such as a Website, Blog or technical documentation…

Contact the Author

Your feedback, comment or technical questions regarding this book can be sent to the following email address:
feedbacks@becomeitexpert.com

You can also:
- Follow the author on Twitter : https://twitter.com/hicham_kadiri
- Connect with him on LinkedIn : https://fr.linkedin.com/in/hichamkadiri
- Connect with him on Viadeo : http://fr.viadeo.com/fr/profile/hicham.kadiri
- Subscribe to his blog : https://hichamkadiri.wordpress.com

Table of contents

Chapter 1. Remote Desktop Services Overview 8
   What is RDS? 8
   What's New in RDS 2012 R2 8
   RDS Terminology 9
   Versions History 10
   Architecture of RDS 2012 R2 10
      RDS 2012 R2 infrastructure components 10
      RDS 2012 R2 Architecture 13
      RDS Limitations 13

Chapter 2. Design your RDS 2012 R2 infrastructure 15
   Hardware and Software requirements 15
   Roles services to deploy 16
   Sizing RDS 2012 R2 infrastructure 16

Chapter 3. Deploy your RDS 2012 R2 infrastructure 18
   RDS 2012 R2 deployment types and scenarios 18
   Setup your Sandbox 20
   Deployment methods 21
      Deploying RDS using Server Manager 21
      Deploying RDS using Windows PowerShell 30
      Deploying RDS using PowerShell Scripts 32

Chapter 4. Create and Manage RDS Collections 34
   What is a RDS Collection? 34
   Create a Session Collection via the Server Manager 36
   Create a Session Collection via Windows PowerShell 40
   Create a Session Collection via PowerShell Script 41
   Configure Settings for your Session Collection 41

Chapter 5. Publish your RemoteApp Programs 49
   Install Apps and Programs on your RDS environment 49
      Install Apps using « CHANGE.exe » 49
      Install Apps using « Install Application on Remote Desktop server » tool 51

Publish your RemoteApp Programs using Server Manager 54

Publish your RemoteApp Programs using Windows PowerShell 58

Publish your RemoteApp Programs using Powershell Script 58

Distribute your RemoteApp Programs 59

    Distribute RemoteApp Programs via the RDWA Portal 59

    Distribute RemoteApp Programs via RDP Files 62

    Distribute RemoteApp Programs via Remote Desktop App 73

Editing RemoteApp Programs properties 77

Publish your Windows Desktops 82

Distribute your Windows Desktop 89

Chapter 6. Manage your RDS 2012 R2 infrastructure 92

Management tools you need to know 92

GUI Management Tools 93

    Server Manager 93

    RD Licensing Diagnoser tool 102

CLI Management Tools 104

    Windows CLI tools 104

    « RemoteDesktop » PowerShell Module 105

RDS Management via Scripts 107

Chapter 7. Secure your RDS 2012 R2 Infrastructure 109

Securing the RD User Environment 109

    Locking Down the RDSH Server 109

    Prevent users from running unwanted applications 112

    Keeping the RD Session Host Server Available 113

    Taking Remote Control of User Sessions: RDS Shadowing 117

Securing RDP Connections 121

    Core Security Features and Technologies 121

    Authenticating RDSH Server Identity (Server Authentication) 122

    How can i set SSL (TLS) security layer for my RDS deployment? 122

    Encrypting RDP Data /Traffic 124

    How can i encrypt RDP traffic? 125

    Authenticating Client Identity with Network Level Authentication (NLA) 127

Chapter 8. Licensing Remote Desktop Services 130

RDS Licensing Model 130

RDS Licensing 130

License Tracking and Enforcement 132

Installing RD License Server 132

RD License Server post-installation tasks 136

    Activate the RD License Server 136

    Add your RD License Server to AD Group 139

    Install the RDS CAL 141

    Configuring RD Session Host Servers to Use RD License Servers 145

    Managing and Reporting License Usage 146

Chapter 9. Make your RDS infrastructure 2012 R2 available from the Internet 148

How RD Gateway Works 148

Understanding RD Gateway Authorization Policies 149

RD Gateway Requirements 151

Installing RD Gateway 151

RD Gateway Server post-installation tasks 156

Chapter 10. Configuring Remote Desktop Services roles for High Availability 171

What is Load Balancing and how it works? 171

Hardware vs Software Load Balancers 171

Configuring HA for RDSH role service 173

Configuring HA for RDWA role service 178

Configuring HA for RDCB role service 192

Configuring HA for RDLS role service 207

Configuring HA for RDG role service 209

Chapter 11. Deploying SSL Certificates 215

Configuring SSL certificate for RD Web Access 220

Configuring SSL certificate for RD Gateway 222

Test your deployment RDS 2012 R2 in Mode HA 225

Chapter 12. Planning for preserving user state 230

Roaming Profiles 230

Folder redirection 231

User Profile Disks (UPD) 231

Enable User Profile Disks 232

Chapter 13. Configuring RDS Universal Printing 237

    Microsoft's Solution: Easy Print 237

    How Easy Print works? 237

    Configuring Easy Print 238

Chapter 14. Configure your RDS 2012 R2 infrastructure using GPO 240

Chapter 15. Customize your RD Web Access Portal 245

    Change the default Workspace name 245

    Change the default Workspace description 246

    Change the default images used by the RD Web Access Portal 247

    Adding the Password Reset feature to RD Web Access 248

Chapter 16. Troubleshoot your RDS 2012 R2 infrastructure 251

    Diagnostic Tools you need to know 251

        Windows Diagnostic Tools 251

        RDS Diagnostic Tool 253

    Windows services used by RDS 253

About the author 256

Chapter 1. Remote Desktop Services Overview

What is RDS?

Formerly **TSE** (Terminal **Se**rvices), **RDS** (**R**emote **D**esktop **S**ervices) is a native role in Windows Server 2012 and 2012 R2.

This is a set of services that enable one or more users to simultaneously access published applications (RemoteApp Programs), Windows Desktop (Remote Desktop Sessions) or Virtual Desktops (VDI), and this via the local corporate network or the Internet.

These resources are accessible via the **RDP** client (Remote Desktop Protocol) and can be distributed via:

- A personalized RDWA Portal
- RDP shortcuts placed on the Windows desktop workstations
- Deployment /integration in the Start Menu or the UI Interface (Welcome Screen since Windows 8)
- "Remote Desktop" App available in Windows Store

The RDS solution consists of 6 role services:

- Remote Desktop **S**ession **H**ost (**RDSH**)
- Remote Desktop **V**irtualization **H**ost (**RDVH**)
- Remote Desktop **L**icense **S**erver (**RDLS**)
- Remote Desktop **C**onnection **B**roker (**RDCB**)
- Remote Desktop **G**ateway (**RDG**)
- Remote Desktop **W**eb **A**ccess (**RDWA**)

Note: *Readers are kindly invited to remember the words quoted above (RDSH, RDWA, RDCB ...) rather than the full names of the role services. These terms will be re-used to facilitate reading of this book.*

What's New in RDS 2012 R2

Remote Desktop Services in Windows Server 2012 R2 brining a lot of new features, including:

- **Session Shadowing**: With this new mode, IT Administrators can now remotely view or take control of Remote Desktop sessions.
- **RDSH Upgrade-In-Place**: The Session Host server can now be upgraded in place (upgrade from RDS 2012 to RDS 2012 R2 only).

- **Support of a Session Host server on a DC:** With RDS 2012 R2, a Remote Desktop Session Host can be deployed on a Domain Controller (DC). And this to allow small businesses benefit from the RDS solution and its features by using the existing servers.
- **Quick reconnect:** In the past, when a network drop caused the client to attempt to reconnect to the remote session or virtual desktop, it could take up to 70 seconds depending on the kind of network the user was on. With RDS 2012 R2, you can be reconnected in less than 10 seconds.

The complete list of new features introduced with RDS 2012 R2 is available at the following URL:

https://blogs.msdn.microsoft.com/rds/2013/07/09/whats-new-in-remote-desktop-services-for-windows-server-2012-r2/

RDS Terminology

Technical terms related to RDS technology are listed in the table below:

Term	Description
RDS	Remote Desktop Services
RDP	Remote Desktop Protocol
TSE	Terminal Services
RD	Remote Desktop
RDC	Remote Desktop Connection
RDSH	Remote Desktop Session Host
RDCB	Remote Desktop Connection Broker
RDWA	Remote Desktop Web Access
RDLS	Remote Desktop Licensing Server
RDVH	Remote Desktop Virtualization Host
RDG	Remote Desktop Gateway
RDG CAP	Remote Desktop Gateway Connection Access Policy
RDG RAP	Remote Desktop Gateway Resource Access Policy
CAL	Client Access License
VDI	Virtual Desktop Infrastructure
NLA	Network Level Authentication
MSI	Microsoft Installer Package
AD DS	Active Directory Domain Services
APP-V	Application Virtualization
SSL	Secure Sockets Layer
SCVMM	System Center Virtual Machine Manager
VMM	Virtual Machine Manager
UPD	User Profile Disks

WSRM	Windows System Resource Manager
DFSS	Dynamic Fair Share Scheduling
GPO	Group Policy Objects
GPMC	Group Policy Management Console
GPEDIT	Group Policy Editor
SQL DB	SQL DataBase
SSMSE	SQL Server Management Studio Express
RDS HA	Remote Desktop Services High Availability
RemoteApp	Remote Application
SSO	Single Sign-On
NLB	Network Load Balancing

Versions History

The Microsoft TSE solution was released first with Windows NT Server.

Indeed, Microsoft proposed a specific Edition of Windows NT Server that included TSE Services: **Windows NT Server Terminal Server Edition**.

However, with Windows Server 2000, TSE components were out of the box with that OS and for all editions

Additionally, with the release of Windows Server 2008, TSE became RDS and all Windows services roles and associated services now carry the RD extension for "Remote Desktop" instead of TS "Terminal Services".

Finally, a new RDS component (role service) was introduced with Windows Server 2008 R2, this is the RDVH. This role service is the essential component of a Microsoft VDI infrastructure.

Architecture of RDS 2012 R2

RDS 2012 R2 infrastructure components

This part describes the different components of the RDS 2012 R2 infrastructure.

 This part also applies to RDS Windows Server 2008 and 2012

⮞ Remote Desktop Session Host

Allows you to manage (accept) multiple Remote Desktop connections simultaneously, it includes the RemoteApp component that allows you to publish and distribute RemoteApp programs.

The Session Host server supports multiple security technologies to secure and encrypt RDP connections and communications.

In addition, it offers an optimized user environment:

- User experience: Windows Themes, Windows 8.1 Tools ...
- Redirection of local resources: local drives, printers, smart cards, audio /video ... etc

⮞ Remote Desktop Virtualization Host

RDVH server integrates with the "Microsoft Hyper-V" to distribute Virtual Desktops (Virtual Machines) on demand

It offers two types of resources:

- Personal VM : assigned to a single user
- VM Pool : assigned to a user group

RDVH role service represents the Microsoft VDI infrastructure.

 The VDI Part (RDVH) is not covered in this Book

⮞ Remote Desktop Licensing Server

Distributes RDS licenses (RDS CALs) Per-User and/or Per-Device to remote users and/or remote computers.

Using "License Manager" snap-in, you can install and manage RDS CALs.

The RDLS server also includes a reporting tool that allows you to export the RDS CAL usage report to .CSV file.

➽ Remote Desktop Connection Broker

Since RDS 2012, Remote Desktop Connection Broker (RDCB), formerly Terminal Services Session Broker (TS Session Broker) is considered as the "Backbone" of RDS infrastructure.

Indeed, the deployment of the RDS role automatically includes the deployment of Service Broker but also RDSH and RDWA servers.

The RDCB is a role service that provides the following functionality:
- Allows users to reconnect to their existing sessions in a load-balanced RD Session Host server farm. This prevents a user with a disconnected session from being connected to a different RD Session Host server in the farm and starting a new session.
- Enables you to evenly distribute the session load among RD Session Host servers in a load-balanced RD Session Host server farm.
- Provides users access to virtual desktops hosted on RD Virtualization Host servers and to RemoteApp programs hosted on RD Session Host servers through RemoteApp and Desktop Connection.

➽ Remote Desktop Gateway

Remote Desktop Gateway (RDG) is a role service that enables authorized remote users to connect to resources on an internal corporate or private network, from any Internet-connected device that can run the Remote Desktop Connection (RDC) client. The network resources can be Remote Desktop Session Host (RD Session Host) servers, RD Session Host servers running RemoteApp programs, or computers with Remote Desktop enabled.

RDG uses the Remote Desktop Protocol (RDP) over HTTPS to establish a secure, encrypted connection between remote users on the Internet and the internal network resources on which their productivity applications run.

➽ Remote Desktop Web Access

Remote Desktop Web Access (RD Web Access), formerly Terminal Services Web Access (TS Web Access), enables users to access RemoteApp and Desktop Connection through the Start Menu or through a Web browser. RemoteApp and Desktop Connection provides a customized view of RemoteApp programs and virtual desktops to users.

Additionally, RD Web Access includes Remote Desktop Web Connection, which enables users to connect remotely from a Web browser to the desktop of any computer where they have Remote Desktop access.

You can customize the RDWA portal to perform the following changes:

- Replace the default logo by the logo of your company or your customer's logo
- Change the title and description of the Portal
- **Add the HelpDesk contact details (@Email and phone number) so that your end users can contact them if needed.**

RDS 2012 R2 Architecture

In a standard RDS architecture, the components mentioned above are deployed as shown in the figure below:

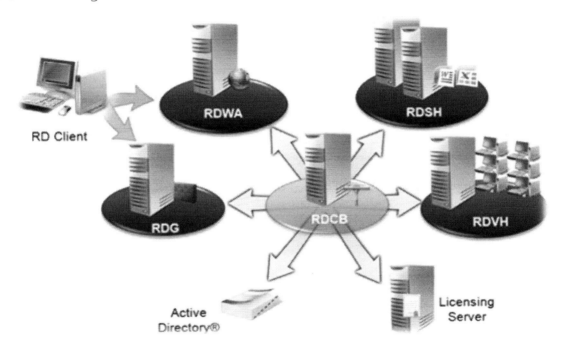

RDS Limitations

According to your Windows Server 2012 R2 Edition, some limitations of RDS exist.

Indeed, all RDS role services are present only on Datacenter, Standard and Foundation editions.

The Essentials Edition only includes the "RD Gateway" role service with some limitations, refer to the table below for more informations:

Server Role	Service Role	Datacenter	Standard	Essentials	Foundation
Remote Desktop Services	Remote Desktop Gateway	✓	✓	⚠ (1)	⚠ (2)

✓ : Available /Full | ⚠ : Available /Restricted

(1) : The RD Gateway is installed /configured automatically. All other RD roles Services are not supported.

(2) : Only 50 remote connections are supported by the RD Gateway.

Chapter 2. Design your RDS 2012 R2 infrastructure

Hardware and Software requirements

➢ Softwares Prerequisites

As explained in the "Introduction", RDS is a native role in Windows Server 2012 R2, the only software prerequisite is Windows Server 2012 R2 installation Media: DVD, ISO image...

Moreover, in large RDS deployment with RDCB HA (High Availability) enabled, you will need Microsoft SQL Server Standard, Enterprise or Express Edition (2008 R2 or higher) that includes SQL Native Client and the SQL Server Management Studio Express (2008 R2 or higher).

➢ Hardware Prerequisites

There is no specific hardware prerequisites for deploying each RDS role service, in fact Microsoft does not provide exact list on TechNet libraries regarding hardware requirements to deploy the RDS role.

RDS requires that the Windows Server 2012 R2 operating system be installed. There are no additional hardware or software requirements for running Remote Desktop Services.

There are several hardware requirements that must be met (on RDSH servers) when you plan to publish several RemoteApp Programs for multiple remote users.

To correctly size your RDSH servers, you must consider the following:

- ➢ Apps (to publish) requirements
- ➢ Number of Apps to publish
- ➢ Number of remote users
- ➢ Types of remote users
- ➢ Network configuration
- ➢ System availability
- ➢ Risk tolerance

E.g: if you want to size your RDSH server(s) that will host three RemoteApp Programs (MS Office Word /Excel /PowerPoint) for 100 remote users, you just have to calculate the amount of Memory and CPU required by each RemoteApp instance and by Remote user (by Session) and then calculate the total amount of RAM/CPU required by each RDSH Server.

The table below details standard prerequisites for each RDS role service, these informations are based on the author's experience and feedbacks following the various RDS projects:

Service role	RAM	vCPU	Disk Space	Network
RDSH	6 GB	4	100 GB	1 GB
RDCB	6 GB	4	60 GB	1 GB
RDWA	4 GB	4	60 GB	1 GB
RDLS	2 GB	2	60 GB	1 GB
RDG	4 GB	4	60 GB	1 GB

Unlike other service roles, the RDSH server must have two partitions: OS (60 GB) and DATA (~40). The data partition is only used for remote app data placeholder.

In a physical infrastructure, RDSH and RDCB servers must have at least Dual Core CPU with 3 GHz. In a small RDS deployment, RDSH/RDCB and RDWA/RDG servers can coexist together.

Roles services to deploy

The person in charge of the RDS deployment project (Project Manager, Consultant or Architect) must consider the following:

Service Role	Description
Remote Desktop Session Host	To host and publish RemoteApp Programs
Remote Desktop Web Access	To make RD resources (RemoteApp Programs & Virtual Desktop) available from a Web Portal
Service Broker	To manage reconnection and load balancing
RDS Gateway	To make internal resources accessible from the outside
Licence Manager	To assign and manage RDS CALs

Sizing RDS 2012 R2 infrastructure

The person in charge of the RDS deployment project should have the answers to the following questions in order to correctly design and size the target RDS infrastructure:

- How many applications do you need to publish?
- Are the applications you want to publish supported on a RDS environment?

- Should the Application be pooled between RDSH servers? If this is the case, two RDSH servers are enough for all the RDS deployment.
- Otherwise, you have to create a Collection for each published Application. Note that each Session Collection requires 2 RDSH servers (for High availability)

→ What is the total number of your remote users?
→ What is the total number of simultaneous connections?
→ What is the total number of simultaneous connections per published Application?
→ Should you limit the number of simultaneous connections per RDSH Server or per published Application?
→ The published applications should be limited to a single instance?
→ What is the access mode? Per User or Device mode (Important for the Licensing RDS)
→ What is the access type? Via the RD Web Access, RDP files (Shortcuts) or the Start Menu/UI Interface
→ Should the RDS infrastructure be accessible to external users?
  - If you plan to allow access for external users, take into account the connection type between your local corporate network and the remote site
  - In addition, the RD Gateway component must be deployed to avoid any connection on the default RDP port (3389).
→ What are the remote devices types: Desktop, Laptop, Tablet, Smartphone
→ A downtime of your RDS infrastructure is tolerable?
  - What is the **M**aximum **T**olerable **D**owntime (MTD)
  - If a downtime is not tolerable, plan to make all the RDS infrastructures components highly available.
→ Should you preserve the remote user state?
  - UPD Feature must be enabled on each Session Collection
  - A local or shared storage will be used?
→ Self-signed SSL certificates can be used?
  - Take into account that the CER file of your SSL certificates can be imported (automatically) via GPO to accelerate the import process for all your clients computers.

Chapter 3. Deploy your RDS 2012 R2 infrastructure

RDS 2012 R2 deployment types and scenarios

New deployment types and scenarios are introduced with RDS 2012 and 2012 R2. The RDS role can now be deployed via two different types and using two different scenarios.

Deployment types

- **Standard deployment** : Deployment of the RDS role services across multiple servers
- **Quick Start** : Deployment of the RDS role services on a single server (Standalone server)

Deployment Scenarios

- **Virtual machine-based desktop deployment** : VDI (Virtual Desktop Infrastructure) > access to published Virtual Desktops and RemoteApps
- **Session-based desktop deployment**: Presentation of Windows Desktop & Apps Publication > access to published RemoteApp programs and session-based desktops.

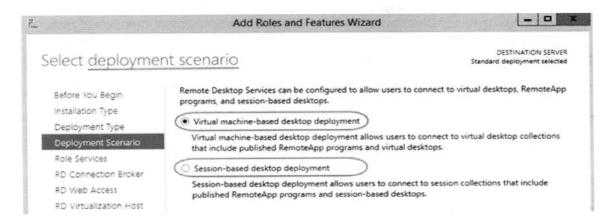

Whatever the deployment type and scenario, at least the three following role services are automatically deployed:

VM-based desktop deployment

- **Remote Desktop Virtualization Host**
- Remote Desktop Web Access
- Remote Desktop Connection Broker

Session-based desktop deployment

- **Remote Desktop Session Host**
- Remote Desktop Web Access
- Remote Desktop Connection Broker

With Windows Server 2012 and 2012 R2, the RDCB is considered as the Backbone of the RDS infrastructure, Microsoft considers that it is essential for the proper functioning of the RDS deployment. This is why a RDS deployment (whatever of the type and deployment scenario) involves the deployment of the RD Connection Broker.

Note that the RDS deployment requires an Active Directory domain.

Setup your Sandbox

➪ Technical informations

Item	Description
DNS Domain Name	BecomeITExpert.Lan
NetBIOS Domain Name	BecomeITExpert
DHCP Enabled	No
Network ID	10.100.10.0
Subnet Mask	255.255.255.0
Primary DNS Server	10.100.10.**10**

The table below details the server configuration informations of our « Sandbox »:

Server #No	Server Role	Host Name	@IP
1	Domaine Controller (DC)	LABDC1	10.100.10.**10**
2	SQL Server Express 2012 SP1	LABSQL1	10.100.10.**11**
3	RDSH	LABRDSH1	10.100.10.**20**
4	RDCB	LABRDCB1	10.100.10.**21**
5	RDWA	LABRDWA1	10.100.10.**22**
6	RDG	LABRDG1	10.100.10.**23**
7	RDLS	LABRDLS1	10.100.10.**24**
8	Client Workstation:Windows 8.1	LABW81	10.100.10.**50**

➪ Sandbox Schema

The following architecture diagram show how are organized the different servers of our Sandbox:

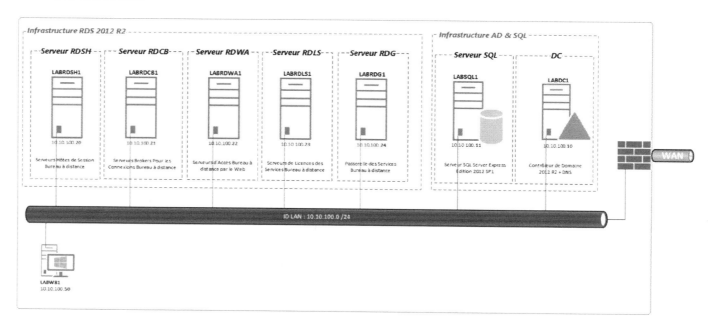

Deployment methods

Remote Desktop Services can be deployed via 3 different methods:

- Using Server Manager
- Using Windows PowerShell (using RemoteDesktop PS Module)
- Using PowerShell Scripts (based on RemoteDesktop PS Module)

Refer to the following sections for more detailed information on each deployment method.

Deploying RDS using Server Manager

Follow the instructions below to correctly deploy the Remote Desktop Services solution via the Server Manager:

- Open a Windows session on the DC « **LABDC1** » and launch the **Server Manager**
- Click on « **All Servers** » > « **Manage** » and then on « **Add Servers** »

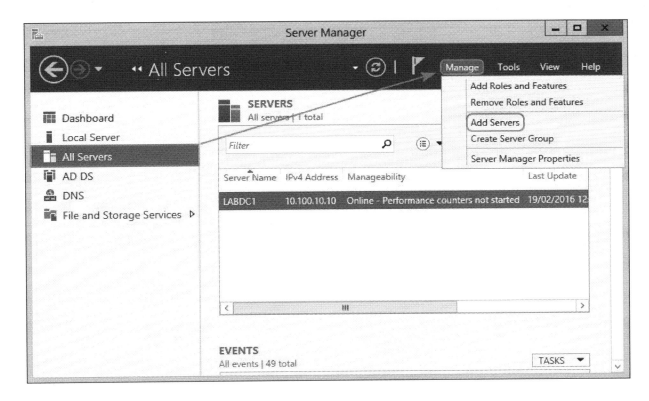

- Locate and add the three servers **LABRDSH1 – LABRDCB1 – LABRDWA1** and click **OK**

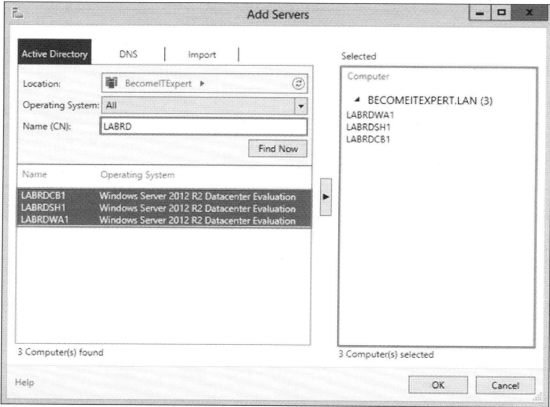

- Once added, the three servers now appear in the « **All servers** » pane

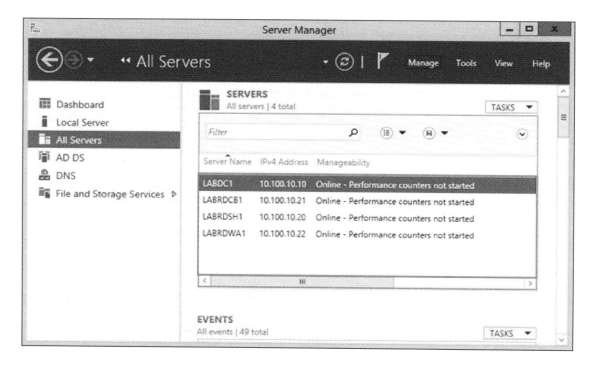

- Now that we've added the servers on which RDS role services will be deployed, go to the Dashboard and click on « **Add roles and features** »:

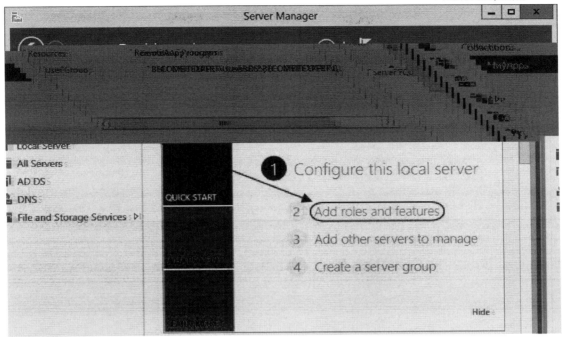

- The « **Add roles and Features** » Wizard is opened, click on « **Next** » to continue

- Select « **Remote Desktop Services installation** » and then click « **Next** »

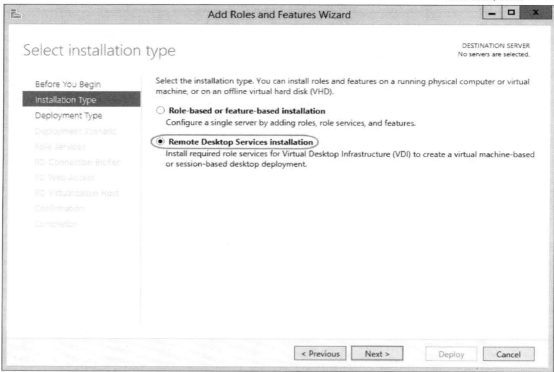

- Select « **Standard deployment** » as a deployment type and click « **Next** »

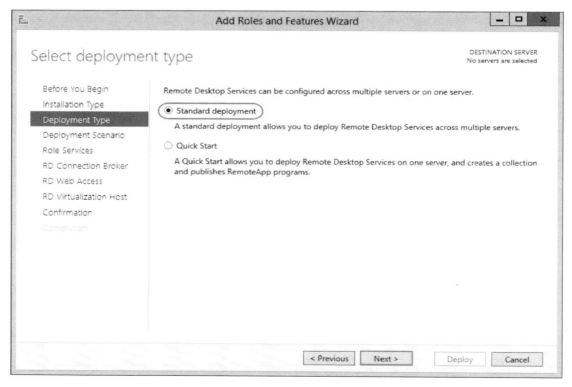

- Select « **Session-based desktop deployment** » as a deployment scenario and click on « **Next** » to continue

- Before clicking on « **Next** » please note the following informations :
  o The three RDS roles service will be deployed as below :
    - Remote Desktop **Session Host** will be deployed on « LABRDSH1 »
    - Remote Desktop **Web Access** will be deployed on « LABRDWA1 »
    - Remote Desktop **Connection Broker** will be deployed on « LABRDCB1 »

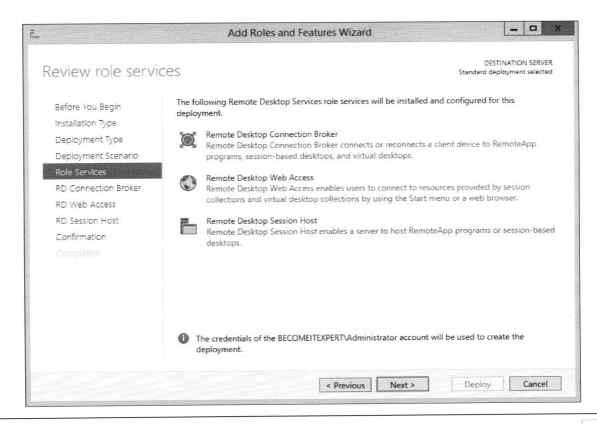

- Select and add the « **LABRDCB1** » server and then click « **Next** »

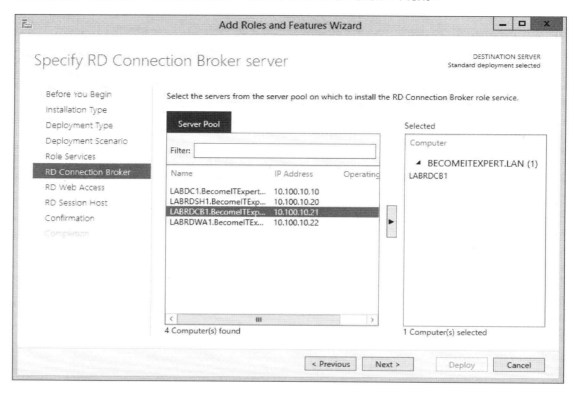

- Select and add the « **LABRDWA01** » server and then click « **Next** »

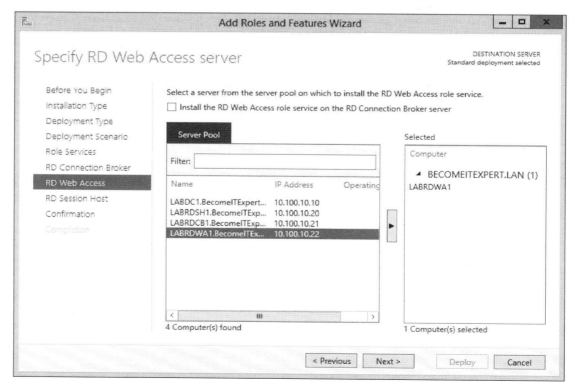

- Select and add the « **LABRDSH01** » server and then click « **Next** »

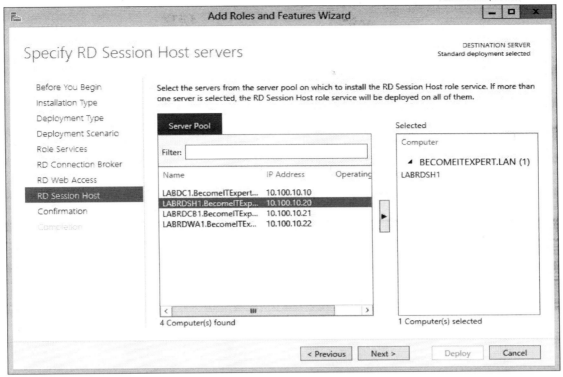

- Tick « **Restart the destination server automatically if required** » and click on « **Deploy** » to start the deployment.
    o *Note: Only the Session Host Server (LABRDSH1) requires a reboot.*

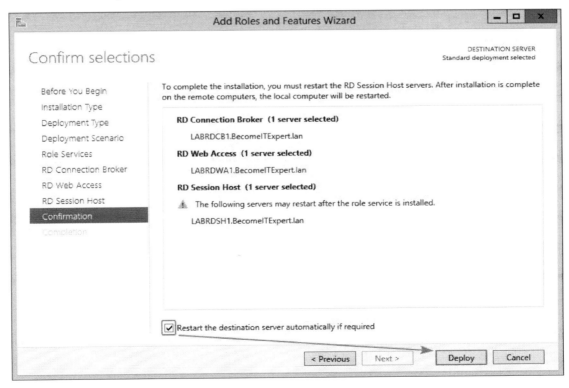

- If your RDS deployment is succeeded, the following informations will be displayed:

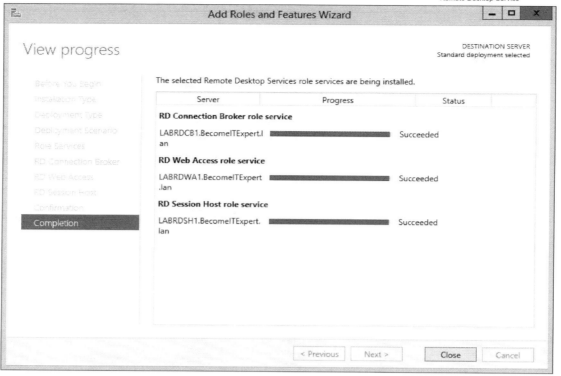

- Click « **Close** » to exit the « **Add Roles and Features** » Wizard.
- You can see that a new management console named **Remote Desktop Services** (or **RDMS**: Remote Desktop Management Server) is now integrated on the left pane of the Server Manager.

 In Windows Server 2012 R2, a single interface (RDMS), replaces all old snap-ins and provides centralized management of the RDS infrastructure. RDMS is a plug-in to the new Server Manager in Windows Server 2012 R2

- Finally, you can test your RDS deployment by connecting to this URL https://RDWA_FQDN/RDWeb, from any machine connected to the network.
- In our case, we will connect to : https://LABRDWA1.BecomeITExpert.LAN/RDWeb from the network machine « **LABW81** »

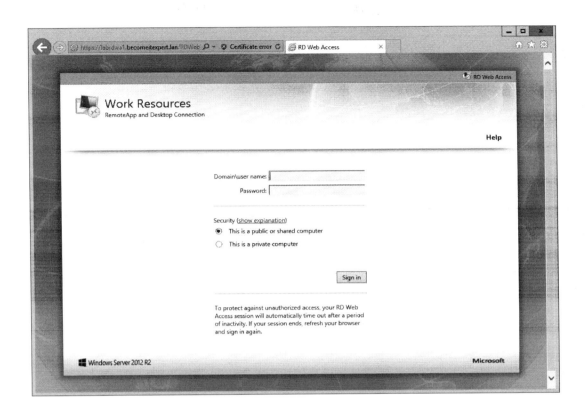

 If you have any constraints about the number of RDS servers to deploy, the three roles services (RDSH, RDCB and RDWA) can be installed on a single server: use the Quick Start mode.

 When using the RDS Quick deployment mode through Server Manager, a default Session Collection is created by default: QuickSessionCollection. In addition, the following three RemoteApp programs are automatically published: WordPad - Paint - Calculator.

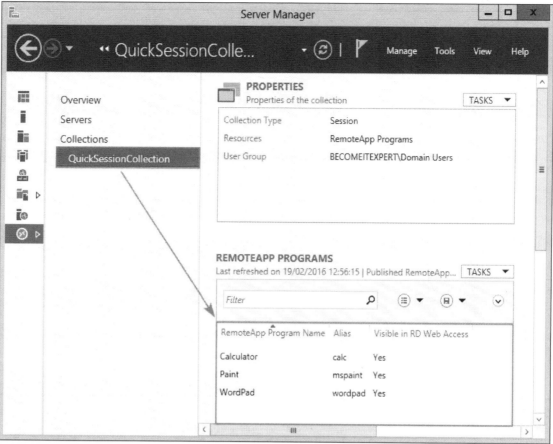

Deploying RDS using Windows PowerShell

To deploy the RDS role services via Windows PowerShell on all servers, you must first enable remote management via Windows PowerShell and set the script execution policy within PowerShell to "**Unrestricted**"

To do this, open a Windows session on each deployed RDS server, launch Windows PowerShell and run the following commands:

    Enable-PSRemoting
    Set-ExecutionPolicy Unrestricted

<u>You are prompted to confirm your choice by entering **Y** for **Yes** or **A** for **All** for both commands.</u>

Follow instructions below to successfully deploy Remote Desktop Services via Windows PowerShell.

Launch Windows PowerShell from DC « **LABDC1** » and type the following commands:

```
Import-Module RemoteDesktop
New-RDSessionDeployment -ConnectionBroker LABRDCB1.BecomeITExpert.LAN
-SessionHost LABRDSH1.BecomeITExpert.LAN -WebAccessServer
LABRDWA1.BecomeITExpert.LAN
```

If you want to deploy RDS in "Quick deployment mode" via PowerShell, just fill in the FQDN of your standalone server with these three parameters: -ConnectionBroker, -SessionHost and -WebAccessServer

Unlike the Quick deployment via the Server Manager, deployement via Windows PowerShell does not create the default Session Collection "QuickSessionCollection" nor the publication of the three test RemoteApp programs: WordPad - Paint – Calculator

After deployment of the RDS role via Windows PowerShell, run the Server Manager from the DC "LABDC1" and check the availability of the RDMS plug-in > « **Remote Desktop Services** »

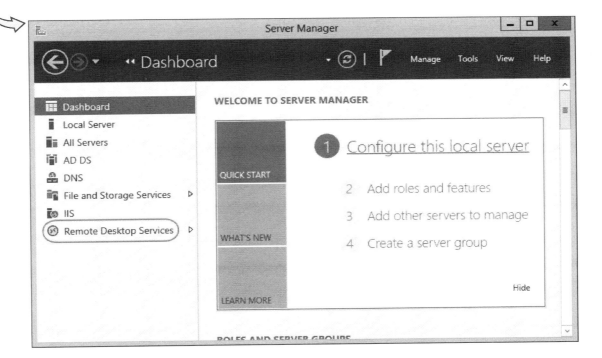

Deploying RDS using PowerShell Scripts

You can also deploy your RDS infrastructure using PowerShell scripts based on the commands used previously.

Script #1 : RDS Quick Deployment Mode (Quick Start)

```
Param (
[Parameter(Mandatory=$TRUE, HelpMessage="Enter the FQDN of your RDS standalone server ")]
[String]
$RDSServer
)

# Import of the RemoteDesktop module
Import-Module RemoteDesktop

# Deploying RDS in Quick Start mode
New-RDSessionDeployment -ConnectionBroker $RDSServer -WebAccessServer $RDSServer -SessionHost $RDSServer
Write-Verbose "RDS Quick Deployment on the server $RDSServer begins"
Write-Verbose "The server $RDSServer requires a reboot so that the RDSH role service can be successfully deployed"

# End of script
```

This script can also be downloaded at the following URL:
https://gallery.technet.microsoft.com/Script-de-dploiement-RDS-0e0bed22

Script #2 : RDS Standard Deployment Mode

```
Param (
[Parameter(Mandatory=$TRUE, HelpMessage="Enter the FQDN of the RDCB server")]
[String]
$RDCB,
[Parameter(Mandatory=$TRUE, HelpMessage="Enter the FQDN of the RDSH server")]
[String]
$RDSH,
[Parameter(Mandatory=$TRUE, HelpMessage="Enter the FQDN of the RDWA server")]
[String]
$RDWA
```

)

Import of the RemoteDesktop module
Import-Module RemoteDesktop

Deploying RDS in Standard mode
New-RDSessionDeployment -ConnectionBroker $RDCB -WebAccessServer $RDWA –SessionHost $RDSH
Write-Verbose "Standard deployment of the RDS role begins on the following servers : $RDCB - $RDSH - $RDWA"
Write-Verbose "The server $RDSH requires a reboot so that the RDSH role service can be successfully deployed

$ End of script

This script can also be downloaded at the following URL:
https://gallery.technet.microsoft.com/Script-de-dploiement-RDS-3599445a

When the RDS role is deployed via the Scripts above, the Server Manager must be closed and restarted so that the new Remote Desktop Services management console appear.

Chapter 4. Create and Manage RDS Collections

What is a RDS Collection?

Collections are a new feature introduced with RDS Windows Server 2012 and 2012 R2.

Collection allows you to group RD Session Host servers into separate farms.

As shown below, Collection 1 groups RDSH1/2 and Collection2 regroups RDSH3/4. This allows you to create a publishing environment for each Department /Activity

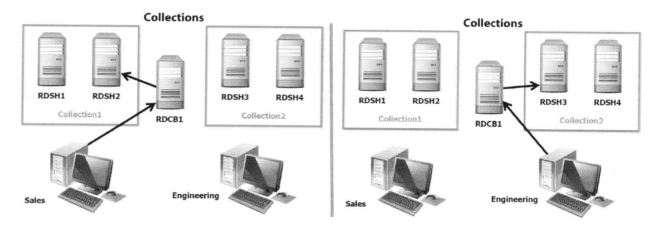

Note that a RDSH server can be part of only one collection at a time.

There are two types of RDS Collection:

- Session Collection
- Virtual Desktop Collection

 Virtual Desktop Collections groups the Virtualization Host Servers (RDVH), this Collection type is not covered in this book.

Session collections can host two types of ressources:

- Remote Desktop
- RemoteApp Programs

By default, after creating a new RDS Session collection, the resource type is defined to "Remote Desktop"

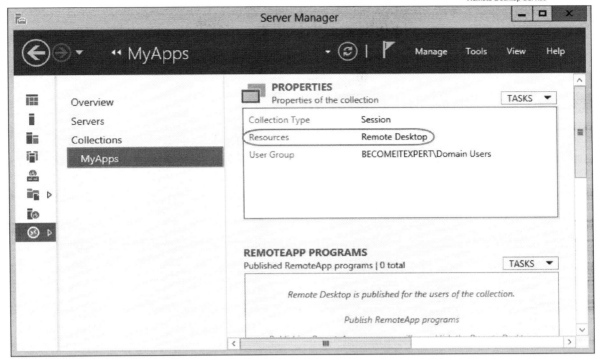

 When you create a quick RDS deployment using Server Manager, the resource type defined on the default Session Collection "QuickSessionCollection" is "RemoteApp Programs" as the 3 test RemoteApp programs are automatically published, see the image below:

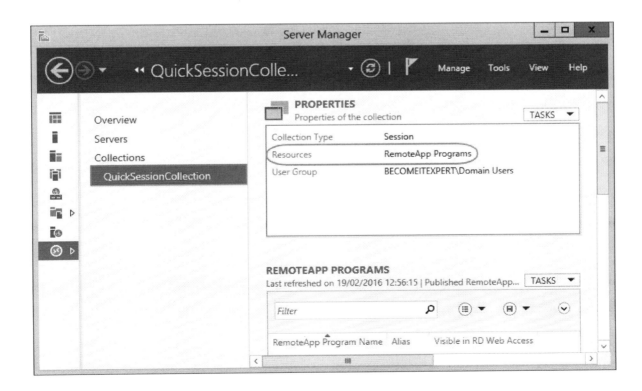

Create a Session Collection via the Server Manager

Follow the instructions below to correctly create a Session Collection via the Server Manager:

- Open a Windows session on DC « **LABDC1** »
- Launch the Server Manager and click on « **Remote Desktop Services** »
- Click on « **Collections** » and select « **Create Session Collection** » under « **TASKS** » :

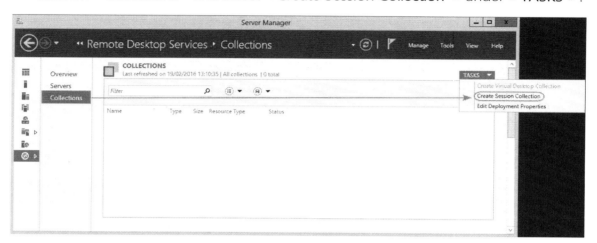

- The « **Create Collection** » Wizard appears, click « **Next** » to continue

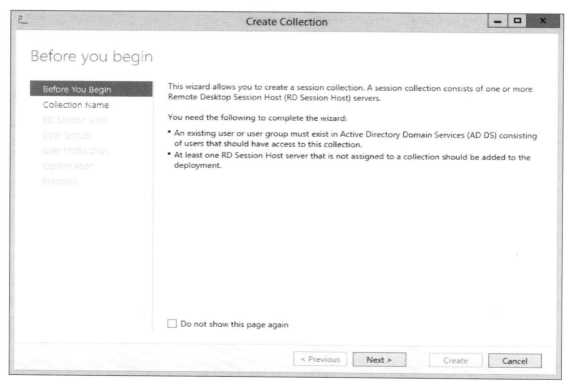

- Fill in the Name and Description of your Session Collection and click « **Next** »

Hicham KADIRI | RDS Windows Server 2012 R2 - Pocket Consultant

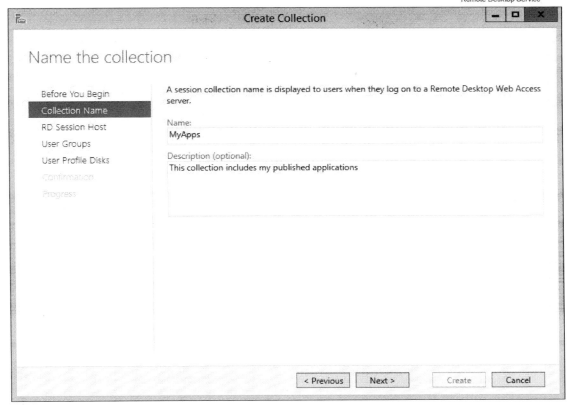

- Select and add « LABRDSH01 » server and then click on « **Next** » to continue

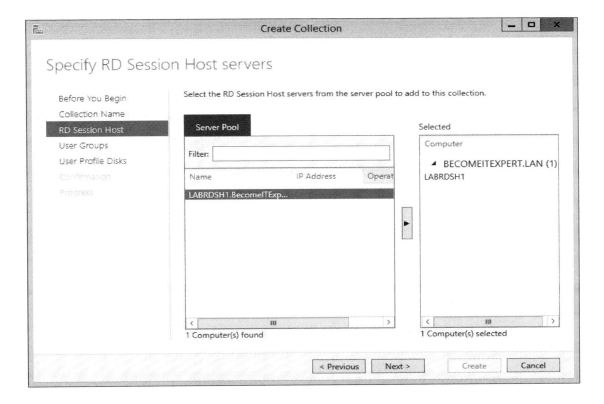

- Leave the default user group « **Domain users** » and click « **Next** »

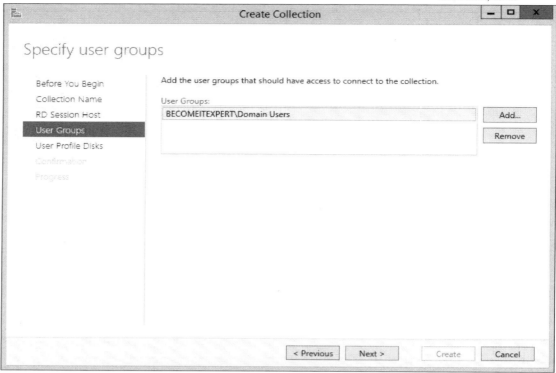

- Uncheck the « **Enable user profile disks** » box and click « **Next** » to continue (we'll discuss this option later in this book)

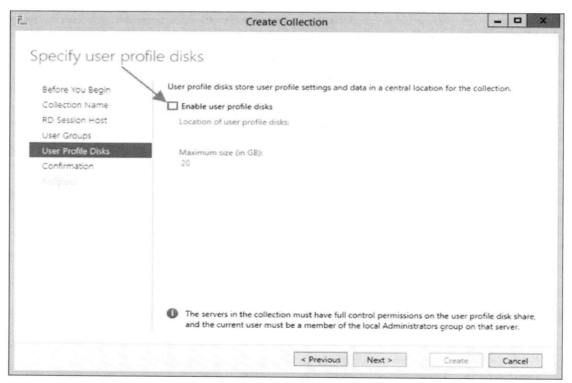

- Check the informations and click « **Create** » to create your Session Collection

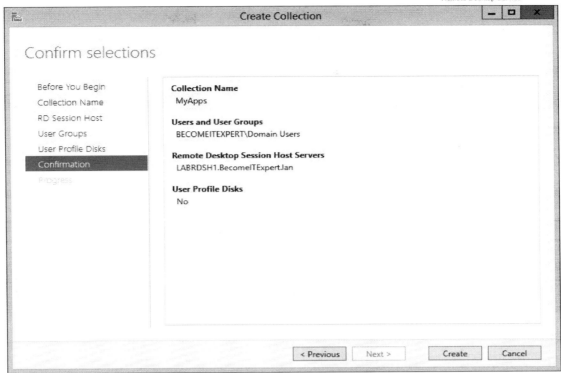

- If your Session Collection has been successfully created, the information below (Succeeded) is displayed

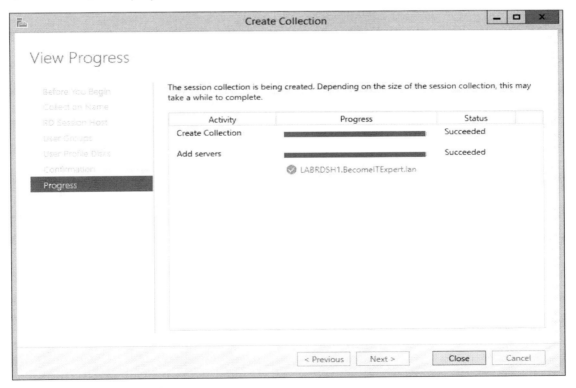

- Click on « **Close** » to exit the « **Create Collection** » Wizard
- Finally, check that the Session Collection you just created is available under the "**Collections**" section

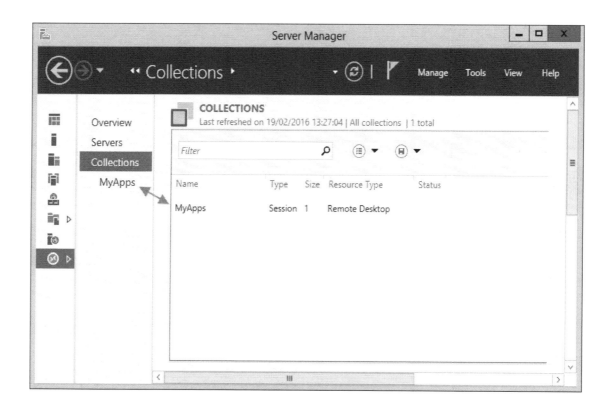

Create a Session Collection via Windows PowerShell

Follow these instructions to successfully create a Session Collection via Windows PowerShell:

- Launch Windows PowerShell from the DC « **LABDC1** » and type the following command:

    Import-Module RemoteDesktop
    New-RDSessionCollection –CollectionName "MyApps" –CollectionDescription "This Collection includes my published applications" –ConnectionBroker LABRDCB1.BecomeITExpert.LAN -SessionHost LABRDSH1.BecomeITExpert.LAN

 You have to close and re-launch the Server Manager to see appear your new "MyApps" Session Collection.

Create a Session Collection via PowerShell Script

You can also create a new Session Collection using a PowerShell script based on the commands used previously.

```powershell
Param (
[Parameter(Mandatory=$TRUE, HelpMessage="Enter the FQDN of the RDCB server")]
[String]
$RDCB,
[Parameter(Mandatory=$TRUE, HelpMessage="Enter the FQDN of the RDSH server")]
[String]
$RDSH,
[Parameter(Mandatory=$TRUE, HelpMessage="Enter the Session Collection name")]
[String]
$CollectionName,
[Parameter(Mandatory=$TRUE, HelpMessage="Enter the Session Collection description ")]
[String]
$CollectionDescription
)

# Import of RemoteDesktop Module
Import-Module RemoteDesktop

# Create a new Session Collection
New-RDSessionCollection  -CollectionName $CollectionName -CollectionDescription $CollectionDescription -SessionHost $RDSH -ConnectionBroker $RDCB
Write-Verbose "The Session Collection $CollectionName is being created..."
```

This script can also be downloaded at the following URL:
https://gallery.technet.microsoft.com/Script-de-Cration-de-e85e559b

Configure Settings for your Session Collection

A Session Collection includes a set of parameters related to RDSH servers, to the Remote Desktop session's security as well as RD client parameters. These can be changed at any time by editing the collection properties.

This section details instructions to follow to correctly modify the settings related to a Session Collection.

In the following example, we'll edit the "MyApps" Session Collection we created previously and make some changes.

To do so:

- Open the Server Manager from the DC « **LABDC1** », click on « **Remote Desktop Services** » and under « **Collections** » select the « **MyApps** » Collection.
- From the right pane and under « **TASKS** », select « **Edit Properties** » :

- The « **MyApps Properties** » dialog box appears
- Under « **General** », you can change the name and description of your Session Collection :

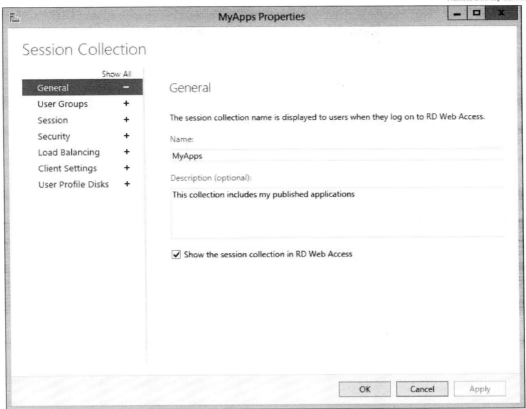

- Under « **User Groups** », you can see that by default, all domain users can access published resources on the "MyApps" Collection, which is strongly not recommended. Microsoft and the author of this book recommends the creation of a dedicated AD security groups to manage access rights to various published resources. In the following example, we will simply specify an AD user group named "**RDSUsers**" instead of the "Domain Users" group , to do this, click the "**Add**" button, then locate and select the "RDSUsers" group you would have previously created, also add the security group "Domain Admins" "and then click "**OK**" to confirm :

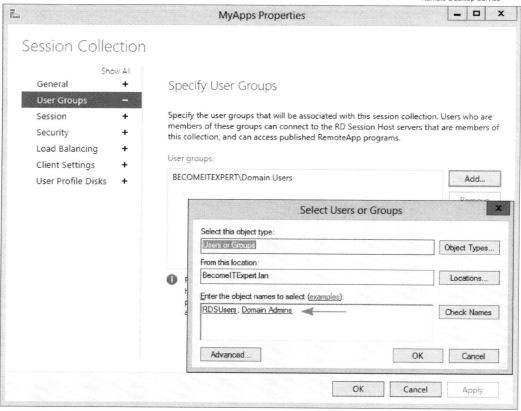

- Once the « **RDSUsers** » user group is added, select and delete the default « **Domain Users** » AD group

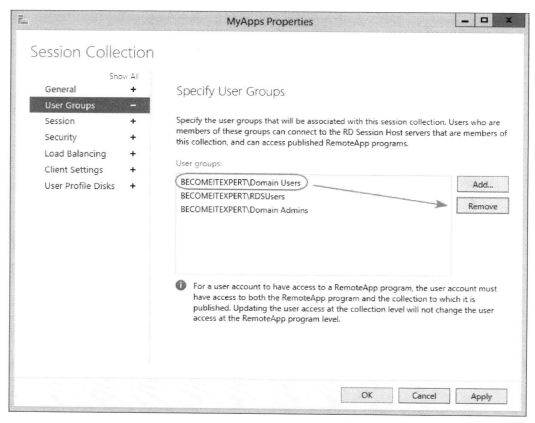

- Under "**Session**" you can configure options related to Remote Desktop Sessions established on RDSH servers which are part of this Session Collection, that includes :
    o Active Session limit
    o Idle Session limit
    o ...

This allows you to optimize and increase RDSH performances.

Note that "**End the Session**" action involves closing all documents and programs currently opened on the remote Session but also the loss of unsaved work of remote users.

"**Disconnect from the session**" action can be used to only disconnect remote users from their Remote Desktop Sessions, their unsaved work (documents and programs) are kept on the server until the next Logon or restart/shutdown of the RDSH server.

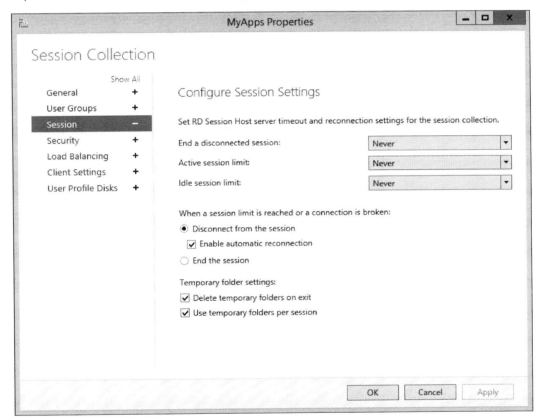

- The "**Security**" section allows you to configure two security options related to Remote Desktop Sessions, including:
    o **The Security Layer** : securing RDP connections
    o **The Encryption Level** : securing RDP communications /Data

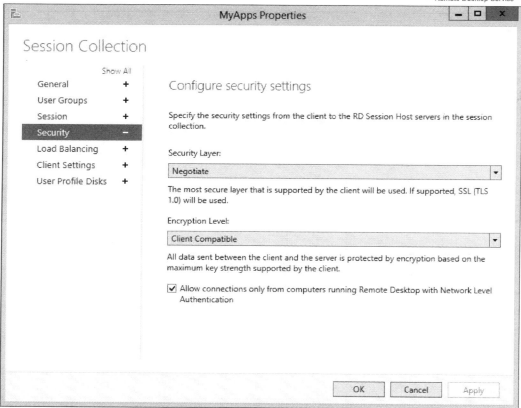

- Under "**Load Balancing**", you can set the load balancing options between the different RDSH servers that are part of the Session Collection, you can also specify a "**Session Limit**" on each RDSH server

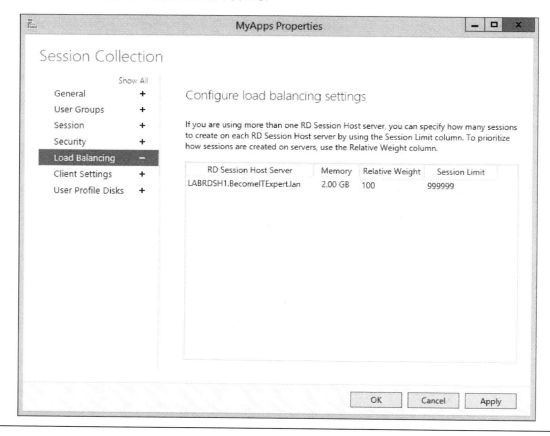

- The "**Client Settings**" section allows you to select local devices and resources to be redirected to the Remote Desktop Sessions, including:
    - Local drives
    - Printers
    - Clipboard (Copy /Paste)
    - SmartCard
    - Audio/Vidéo
    - ...

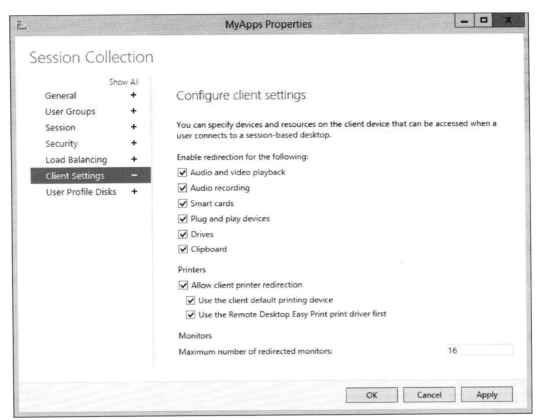

- Under "**User Profile Disks**" you can enable or disable a user profile disks option (UPD), this is a new RDS 2012 /2012 R2 feature, this option allows you to enable persistent profiles data of your remote users (Refer to Chapter 12. Planning for preserving user state for more informations).

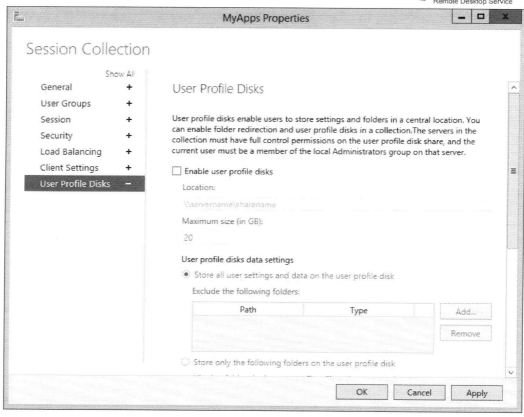

Chapter 5. Publish your RemoteApp Programs

Install Apps and Programs on your RDS environment

There are two tools you can use to install Apps and Programs you need to publish:

- **CHANGE.exe** command line tool
- **Install Application on Remote Desktop Server** tool (Control Panel Tool)

Install Apps using « CHANGE.exe »

By default, RDSH servers are in « **Application EXECUTE** » mode, you can check it by typing « **Change User /Query** » from the Command Prompt or Windows PowerShell:

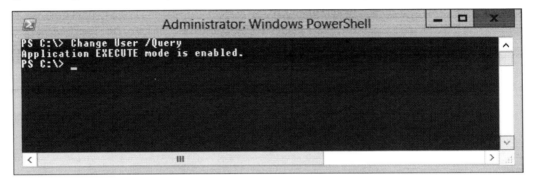

To install the applications /programs you need to publish, the RDSH server must be in « **Application INSTALL** » mode

To do so, run the Command Prompt (cmd.exe) or Windows PowerShell (as Administrator) from your RDSH server and type the following command:

Change User /Install

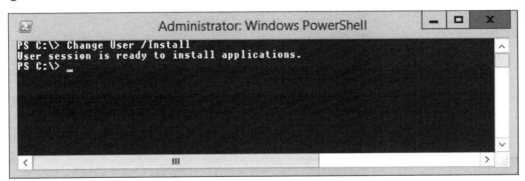

Once the Install mode is set on your RDSH server, you just have to run the Setup file (Setup.exe) of the application you want to publish and perform a typical installation (next, next ... Finish).

In the following example, Microsoft Word /Excel /PowerPoint (2013) will be our first RemoteApp Programs that will published.

- Mount the Microsoft Office 2013 ISO Image and run the Setup.exe file :

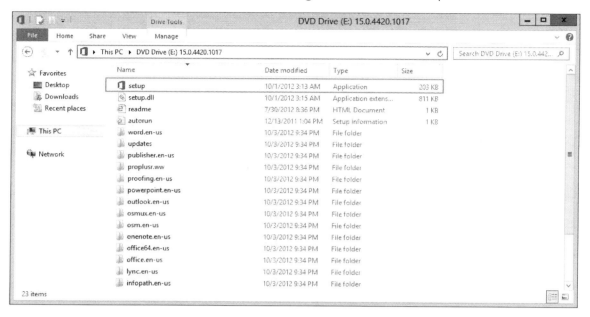

- As mentioned earlier, only Word, Excel and PowerPoint will be installed:

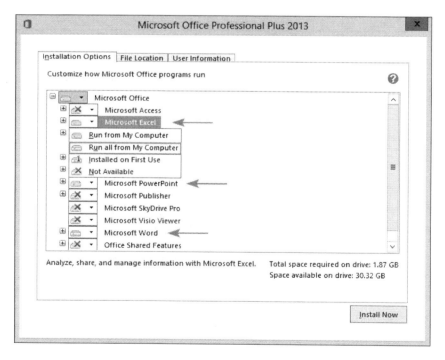

- Once installed, click « **Close** » to exit the Wizard :

The RDSH server must now be back on "**Application EXECUTE**" mode, and this by using the following command from cmd.exe or Windows PowerShell run as Administrator, type:

Change User /Execute

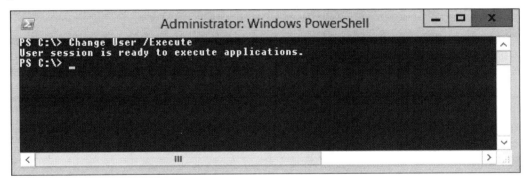

Install Apps using « Install Application on Remote Desktop server » tool
You can also install the Apps you need to publish by using a native tool in Windows Server 2012 and 2012 R2, it's available from the Control Panel and named "**Install Application on Remote Desktop Server**". The use of this tool also requires the configuration of the RDSH server in the correct mode. In fact the tool includes commands to set (automatically) the RDSH server in:

- Installation Mode : Before installing the application to publish
- Execution Mode : After installing the application to publish

Follow the instructions below to install your applications using "**Install Application on Remote Desktop Server**" tool:

- From the Control Panel, click on "**Install Application on Remote Desktop Server**":

- The following Wizard appears, click « **Next** » to continue :

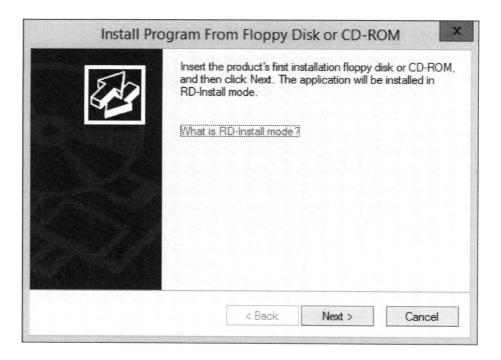

- Click the "**Browse...**" button, locate and select the setup file (.exe file) of your application /software and then click "**Next**" to continue:

- The installation wizard of your Application is launched. Follow the wizard to perform a typical installation of your application.
- In the following example, "**Notepad ++**" will be installed:

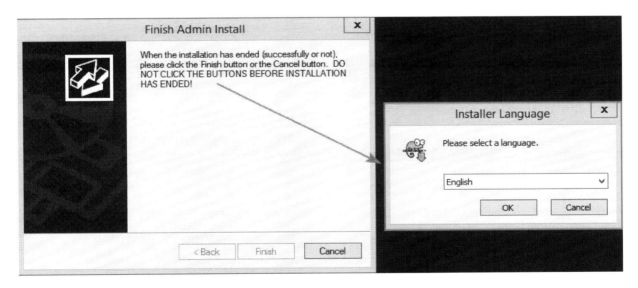

- Once installed, click "**Finish**" to close the wizard:

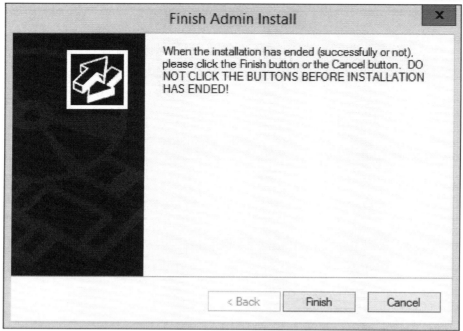

Repeat this operation for each application or software you want to publish.

The following sections will cover all technical method and tools that allow you to publish your RemoteApp Programs.

With RDS Windows Server 2012 and 2012 R2, RemoteApp Programs can be published via three different methods:

- Manager Server
- Windows PowerShell
- PowerShell Script

Publish your RemoteApp Programs using Server Manager

Follow the instructions below to successfully publish your RemoteApp programs via the Server Manager:

- Launch the Server Manager from the DC « **LABDC1** »
- Click on "**Remote Desktop Services**" console and then « **MyApps** »
- As shown in the image below, there are two options that allow you to publish your RemoteApp Programs:
    - Under **TASKS** > **Publish RemoteApp Programs**
    - **Publish RemoteApp program** button that's available under the « **REMOTEAPP PROGRAMS** » section

 Note that after the publication of the first RemoteApp program, the second option will be no longer available

- Both options launch the "**Publish RemoteApp Programs**" Wizard.
- Once the "Publish RemoteApp Programs" Wizard is launched, it will check all available RemoteApp Programs hosted on the RDSH Server(s) that are part of the Session Collection.
- As shown below, we will select Excel 2013, PowerPoint 2013 and Notepad++:

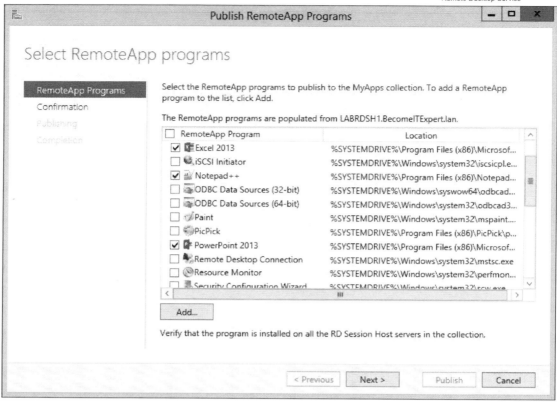

- Make sure the 3 RemoteApp Programs selected are listed above and click on « **Publish** » :

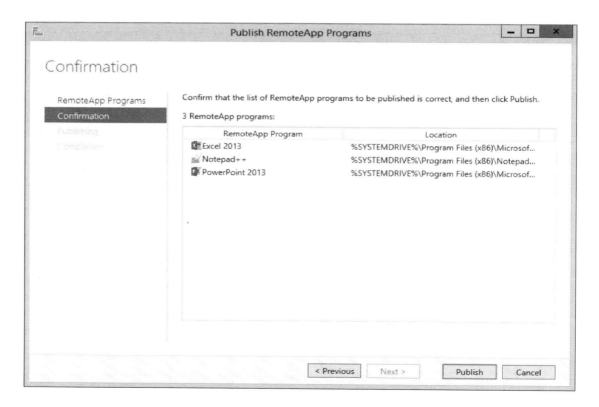

- Finally, click "**Finish**" to close the wizard:

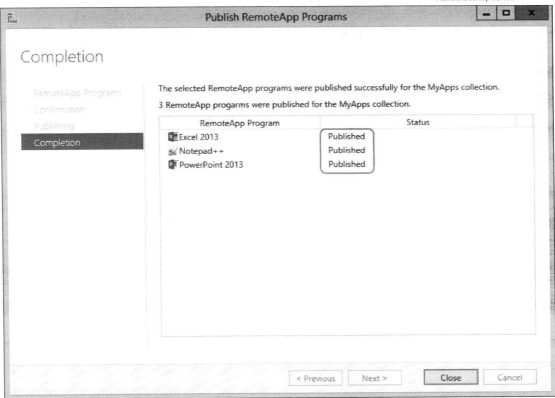

Note that when publishing the RemoteApp programs through the Server Manager, they are automatically visible in the RD Web Access portal:

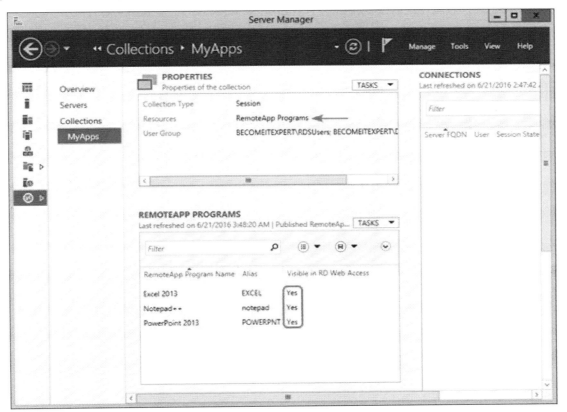

Publish your RemoteApp Programs using Windows PowerShell

Follow the instructions below to successfully publish your RemoteApp programs via Windows PowerShell:

- Open a Windows Session on the RDSH server « **LABRDSH1** », run Windows PowerShell as Administrator and then type the following command:
  - *Note : In the following example, we will publish the RemoteApp program "Word 2013" previously installed :*

```
Import-Module RemoteDesktop
New-RDRemoteApp –Alias "Word" –DisplayName "Word2013" –FilePath "C:\Program Files\Microsoft Office\Office15\WINWORD.EXE" –ShowInWebAcces 1    –CollectionName "MyApps" –ConnectionBroker LABRDCB1.BecomeITExpert.LAN
```

 The value "**1**" of the parameter "-**ShowInWebAccess** " make your published RemoteApp Program visible in RD Web Access, if it should be hidden, the value of this parameter must be set to **0**

Publish your RemoteApp Programs using Powershell Script

You can also publish your RemoteApp Programs by using the PowerShell Script below

```
Param (
[Parameter(Mandatory=$TRUE, HelpMessage="Enter the FQDN of the RDCB server ")]
[String]
$RDCB,
[Parameter(Mandatory=$TRUE, HelpMessage="Enter the Collection name")]
[String]
$CollectionName,
[Parameter(Mandatory=$TRUE, HelpMessage="Enter an Alias for the RemoteApp Program"]
[String]
$RemoteAppAlias,
[Parameter(Mandatory=$TRUE, HelpMessage="Enter a Display Name for the RemoteApp Program")]
[String]
$RemoteAppDisplayName,
[Parameter(Mandatory=$TRUE, HelpMessage="Enter a RemoteApp Program path")]
[String]
$RemoteAppPath
)
```

```
# Import of module RemoteDesktop
Import-Module RemoteDesktop
# Publication of the RemoteApp Program
New-RDRemoteApp -Alias $RemoteAppAlias –DisplayName $RemoteAppDisplayName
-FilePath $RemoteAppPath -ShowInWebAccess 1 -CollectionName $CollectionName
-ConnectionBroker $RDCB
Write-Verbose "The RemoteApp Program $RemoteAppDisplayName is being published ..."
```

Distribute your RemoteApp Programs

Once published, the RemoteApp programs can be distributed via three methods:

- ➔ RD Web Access Portal
- ➔ RDP Files (Manually copy RDP files Shortcuts):
  - Placed on the "Start Menu" or "Welcome Screen" on Windows 8 /8.1"
  - Placed on remote user's Windows Desktop
- ➔ The Modern "Remote Desktop" App available on Windows Store

Distribute RemoteApp Programs via the RDWA Portal

After you publish your RemoteApp Programs through the methods mentioned above, they automatically become visible and accessible from the RDWA Portal:

- From « **LABW81** » client, open Internet Explorer and type :
  https://LABRDWA1.BecomeITExpert.LAN/RDWeb
- Ignore the error message below and click "**Continue to this website** ..." this is a SSL certificate issue, we'll explain later in this Book how to fix it:

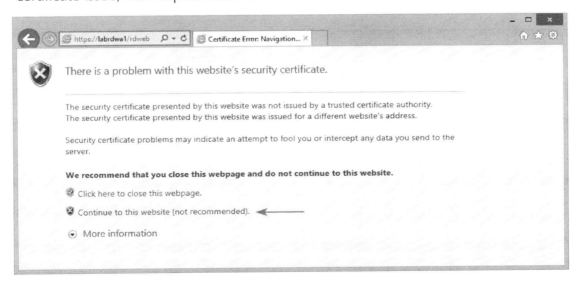

- Fill in with your user name and password and then click « **Sign in** » :

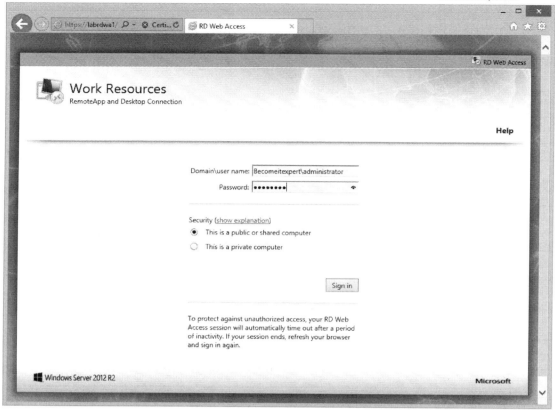

- The RemoteApp Programs to which you have access appear, click on a RemoteApp program to launch it (Excel in the example below):

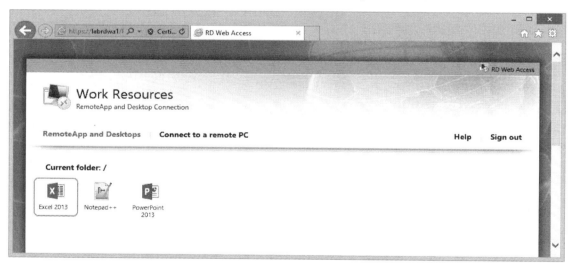

- "Excel 2013" is starting, ignore the error message and click "**Connect**"

- Enter your password and click « **OK** »
- If your RDS deployment is correctly deployed, Excel is started and the following RemoteApp Window appears:

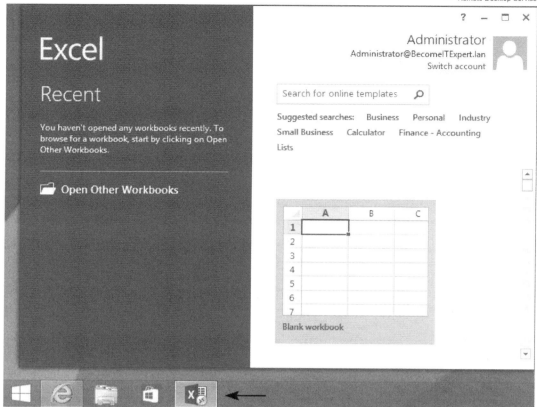

Distribute RemoteApp Programs via RDP Files

RemoteApp Programs can also be distributed by integrating RDP files on remote user's workstations, there are two integration options:

- Start Menu Integration : Integration of RDP files on the Start Menu (or Welcome Screen on Windows 8 and 8.1)
- Windows Desktop Integration : Integration of RDP files on remote user's Desktop (RDP Shortcuts)

Option #1: Start Menu Integration

Since the debut of RemoteApp in Windows Server 2008, Windows users have been able to enjoy remote applications with the same look and feel as local applications. Microsoft provides a native tool called "**RemoteApp and Desktop Connections**" in Windows 8 /Windows Server 2012 and Windows 8.1 /Windows Server 2012 R2 that builds on this by bringing RemoteApp Programs to the Start Menu, giving them the same launch experience as local applications.

Note that the use of this tool requires the presence (import) of the RD Web Access SSL certificate on the remote desktop's machine.

We'll first see how to import the RDWA SSL certificate into certificates store of our network machine "**LABW81**" and then configure the "RemoteApp and Desktop Connections" tool to connect and bring RemoteApp Programs to the Start Menu of our Windows 8.1 client

Follow the instructions below to import the RDWA SSL certificate into the Certificate Store of « **LABW81** » client:

- From the RDWA Portal, click on "**Certificate Error**" as shown in the image below:

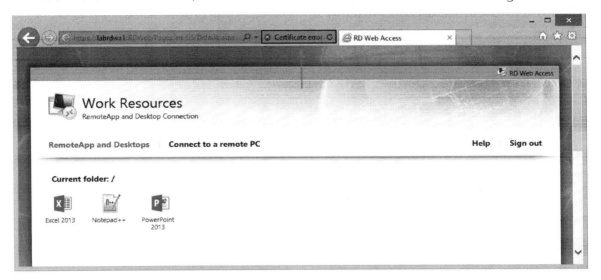

- Click on « **View certificates** »

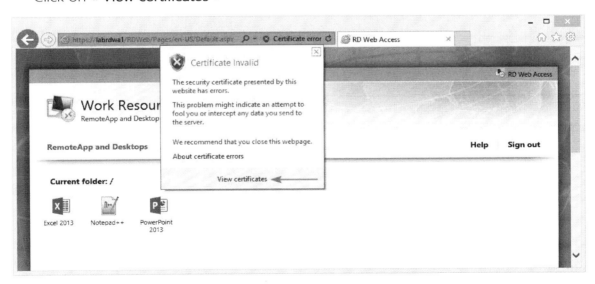

- Finally, click on « **Install Certificate...** »

- Select « **Local Machine** » and then click « **Next** » to continue :

Note: this action requires administrator privileges

- Select "**Place all certificates in the following store**" and click "**Browse...**":

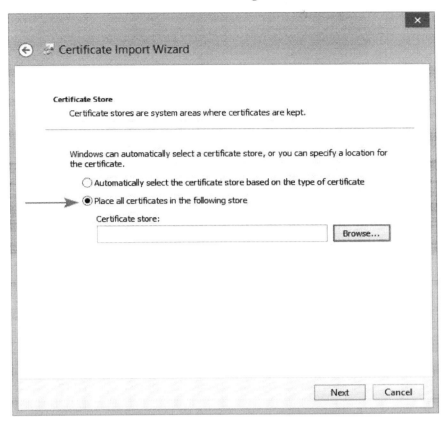

- Select "**Trusted Root Certification Authorities**" and click « OK » :

- Click « **Next** » to continue :

- Click « **Finish** » to exit the "Certificate Import Wizard":

- If the certificate has been correctly imported, the following message appears, click « OK » :

- After importing the SSL certificate, the error message disappears from the Internet Explorer address bar. Note that you must close and re-open Internet Explorer and then re-establish a new connection to the RDWA portal URL to see the new change:

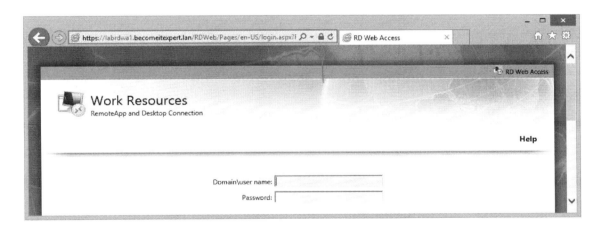

Now that the SSL certificate has been imported, we can integrate RemoteApp programs in the Welcome Screen of our client "**LABW81**" via the « RemoteApp and Desktop Connections » tool, to do so:

- Open a Windows Session on "**LABW81**" client using a Domain Administrator account or a user account member of the "RDSUsers" user group, previously defined on the "**MyApps**" Collection
- Open the Control Panel and click on "**RemoteApp and Desktop Connections**":

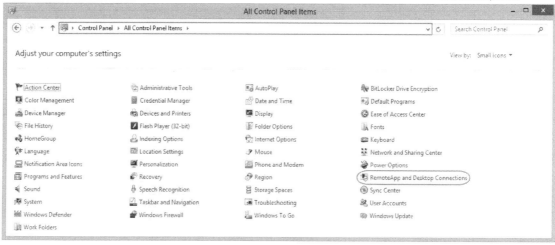

- Click on "**Access RemoteApp and desktops**":

- Type : https://LABRDWA1.BecomeITExpert.LAN/RDWeb/Feed/webfeed.aspx and click « **Next** »:

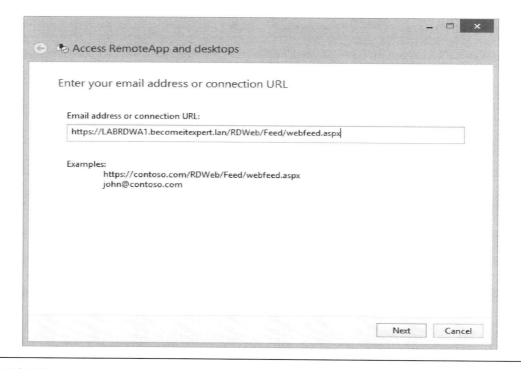

- Click « **Next** » to continue :

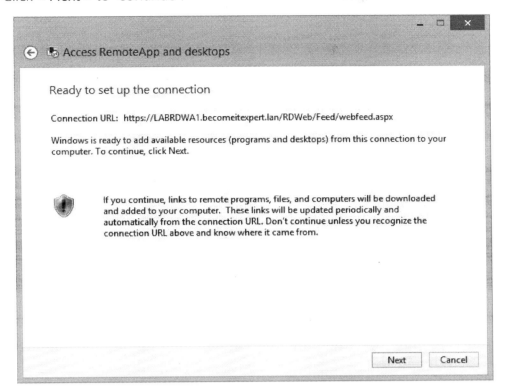

- Type your username and password and click « **OK** » :

- The RemoteApp Programs (and Desktops) retrieved are displayed under "**Programs available**" (and Desktops available), click "**Finish**" to close the "Access RemoteApp and desktops" wizard :

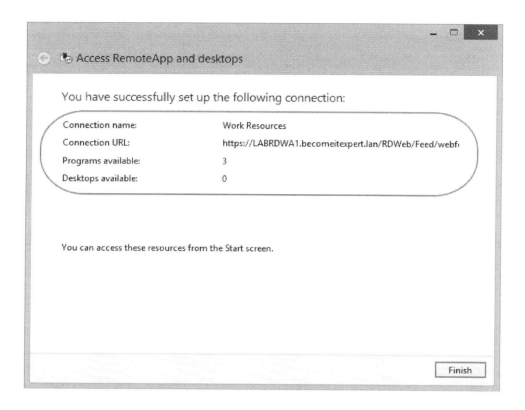

- The "RemoteApp and Desktop Connections" tool now displays informations about the Remote Desktop Workspace to which you are connected and also about the published RemoteApp programs to which you have access:

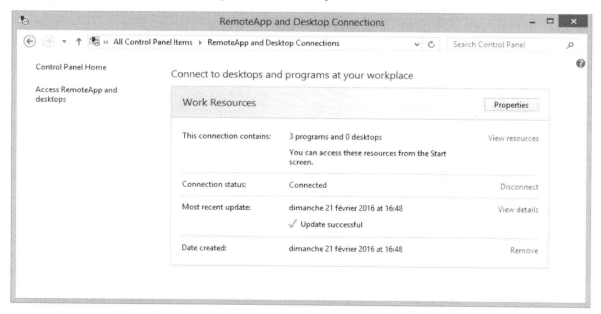

In addition, a new icon appears on the notification bar, it is displayed when the connection to the RD workspace is established.

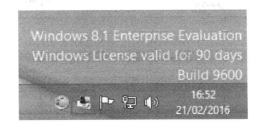

- Finally, click the "**Start**" button and check the integration of the 3 new RemoteApp Programs previously retrieved:

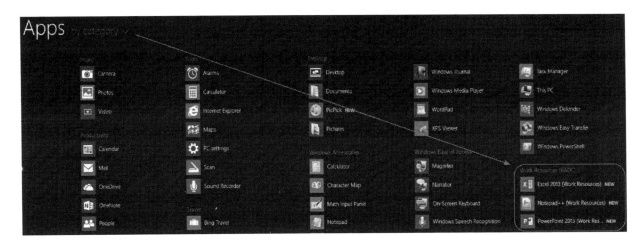

➔ Option #2 : Windows Desktop Integration

After integration of RemoteApp Programs on the Start Menu, their associated RDP files are automatically placed in a subfolder with the same name as the RD Workspace (Work Resources by default), this subfolder is placed in:
C:\Users\%UserProfile%\AppData\Roaming\Microsoft\Windows\Start Menu\Programs\

The instructions below explain how to retrieve the RDP files and place them on the Windows desktop:

- Open the control panel, click on «**RemoteApp and Desktop Connections**» and then click on «**View resources**»:

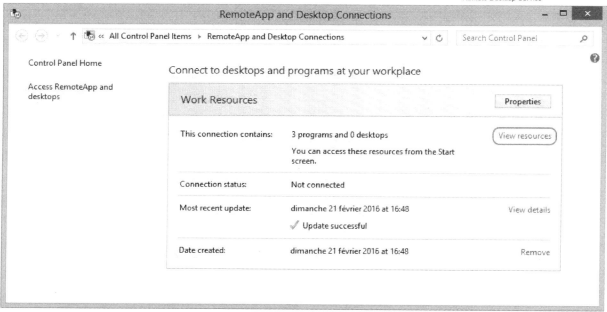

- Copy RDP files of the RemoteApp Programs you want to place on the Windows desktop:

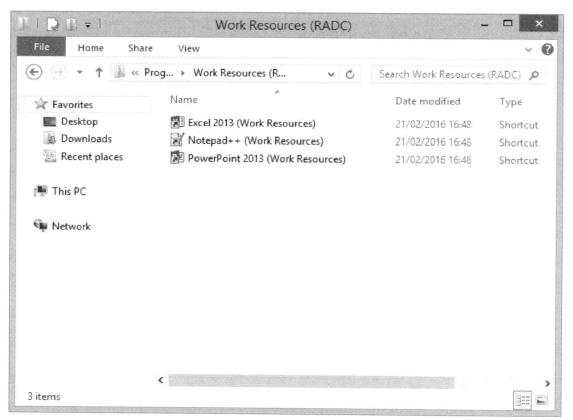

- Put/Paste RDP files on the desktop and rename them if necessary :

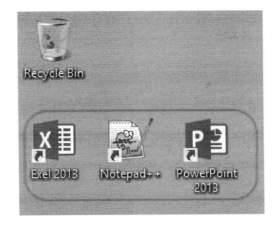

Distribute RemoteApp Programs via Remote Desktop App

The third method you can use to distribute your RemoteApp programs is a Microsoft Application available from Windows Store: **Remote Desktop**.

To download this application you must use a Microsoft account (Hotmail, Live, Xbox Live ...) to be able to log on Windows Store.

The "Remote Desktop" application is also available for free download from the Windows Store website:

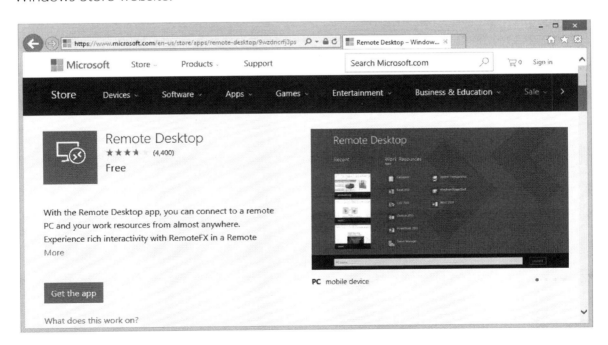

Follow the instructions below to install "**Remote Desktop**" application and configure it to distribute your RemoteApp programs:

- Open a Windows session with a local user account on the client « LABW81 »
- Connect to your Microsoft account and run Windows Store

- Type "**Remote Desktop**" on the search box and confirm your search: :
- Click « **Install**» :

Remote Desktop

Install

Free ★★★★ 3,249

When you install an app, you agree to the Terms of Use and any additional terms.

This app has permission to use some features of your PC that might affect your privacy.

- Once installed, go to the Welcome Screen, make sort by "**date installed**" and verify the availability of the "Remote Desktop" application

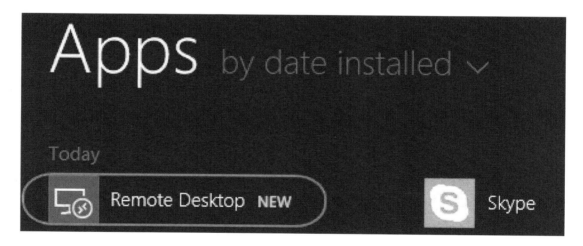

- Click on "**Access RemoteApp and Desktop Connections**"

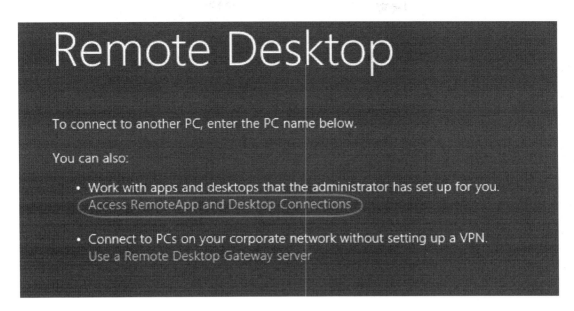

- Type the RDWA's URL followed by **/Feed/webfeed.aspx** and click "**Connect**"

- Enter your user account and its associated password and click **OK**.

 You can tick "Remember my credentials" box to save your credentials for any future connection

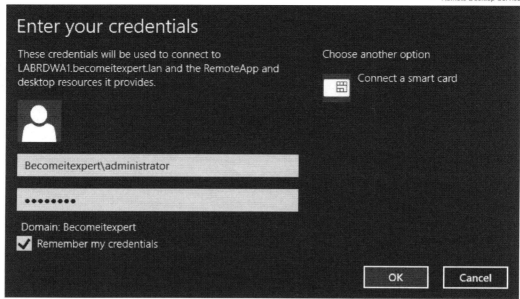

- The number of RemoteApp programs (and Desktops) available is displayed, click **OK** :

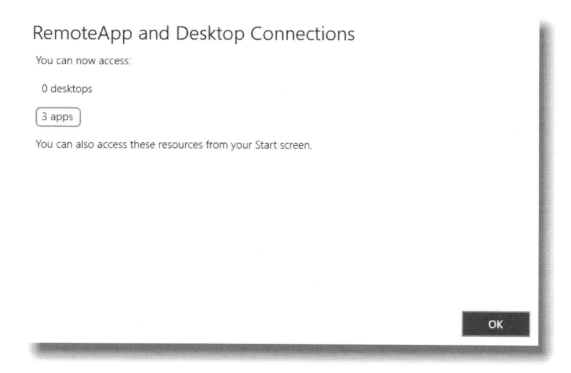

- All retrieved RemoteApp programs now appear in the application "**Remote Desktop**":

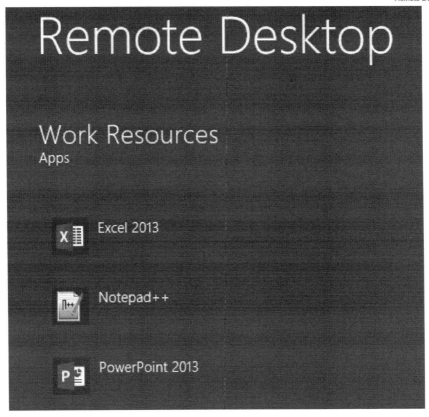

Editing RemoteApp Programs properties

Once published, RemoteApp programs can be edited to configure a set of parameters that allow you to:

- ➡ Change the RemoteApp Program name
- ➡ Make (or not) your RemoteApp Program visible in RDWA Portal
- ➡ Organize /place RemoteApp program in a specific Folder
- ➡ Specify command-line arguments prior to launch the RemoteApp Program
- ➡ Configure the user assignment for RemoteApp programs to limit visibility to a specific user or user groups
- ➡ Associate file types (file extensions) to Program RemoteApp

Just right-click on the published RemoteApp program and select "**Edit Properties**" to launch the "**Properties**" dialog box.

In the following example, the Properites of Excel2013 will be edited.

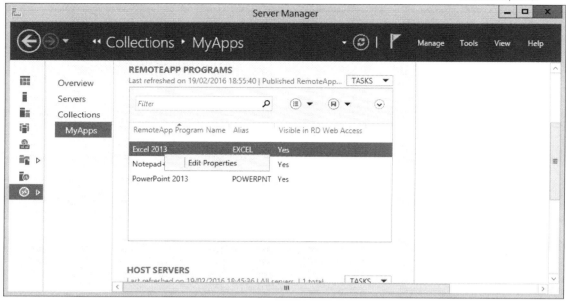

The "**General**" pane lets you change the RemoteApp program name, make or not the RemoteApp program in visible in RDWA portal and also choose a RemoteApp Program folder.

That last option is very useful if you want to organize and place your RemoteApp programs in specific Folders (depending on the application type, department ...Etc):

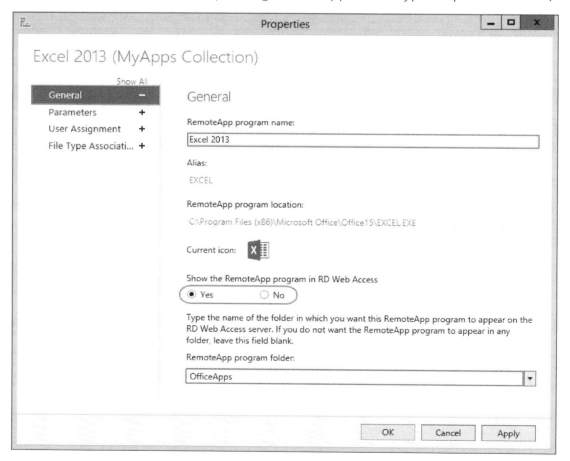

The "**Parameters**" pane lets you specify command-line parameters to start with your RemoteApp program, for example you can publish the RDC client (Remote Desktop Connection) which corresponds to the MSTSC.exe tool and specify the command line parameter /V: LABRDSH1 to connect directly to LABRDSH1 server while launching this RemoteApp program:

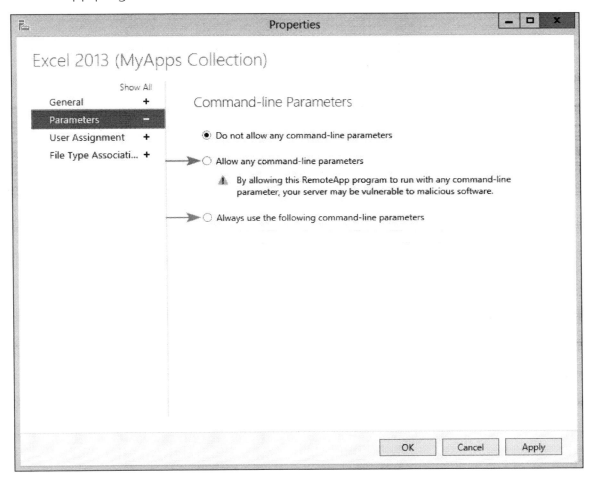

The "**Users Assignment**" pane allows you to limit the visibility of the RemoteApp program to a specific user or users group. This can be useful if you have any constraints about the number of RDSH Server to deploy, you can add all users group on the collection and limit visibility for each RemoteApp program only to a specific user and/or user groups, this method allows you to limit the number of the dedicated RDSH Server per Collection.

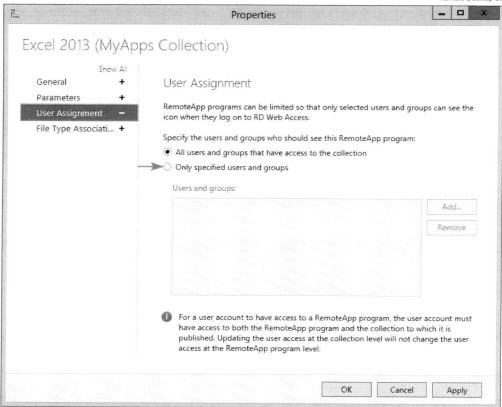

The last pane "**File Type Associations**" lets you configure the various file types that can be associated and opened with the published RemoteApp programs, in our example, Excel can be associated with the files extensions: .XLS, .XLSX, .ODS ...

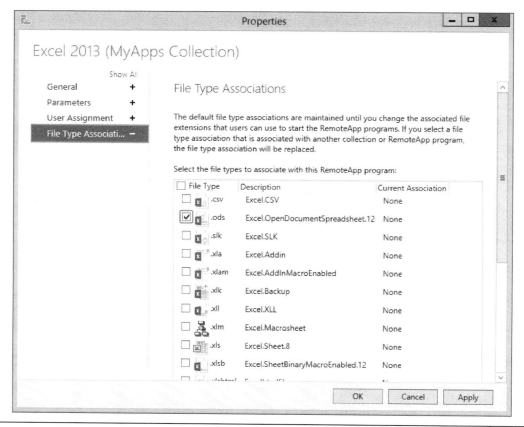

 As a practical workshop, place the RemoteApp programs "Excel - PowerPoint" in "**OfficeApps**" folder and Notepad ++ in "**DevApps**" folder. The result should look like the image below :

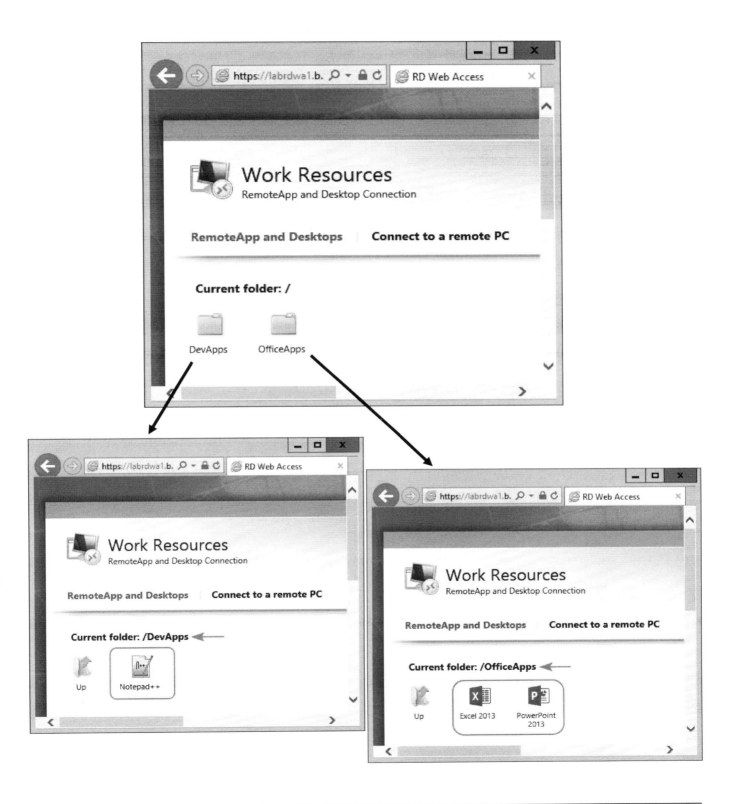

Publish your Windows Desktops

The second resource type that you can publish into Session Collection is Windows Desktop.

The Windows Desktop publishing method is different from the RemoteApp programs, however the different distribution methods remain the same.

Follow the instructions below to successfully create a new Session Collection on which LABRDSH2's Windows Desktop will be published.

 You must have a second RDSH server for that new Session Collection, as mentioned earlier in this Book, a RDSH server cannot be part of two collections at a time. In the following example a new RDSH server named "LABRDSH2" was deployed and joined to our AD domain

- Open a Windows session on DC "**LABDC1**" and launch the Server Manager

- Add the new RDSH server "**LABRDSH2**" to Servers Pool (from the "**All servers**" pane)

- Click on "**Remote Desktop Services**" and then "**Overview**"

- Under "**DEPLOYMENT OVERVIEW**", right-click on "**RD Session Host**" and select "**Add RD Session Host Servers**"

- Select and add the server "**LABRDSH2**", then click "**Next**" to continue:

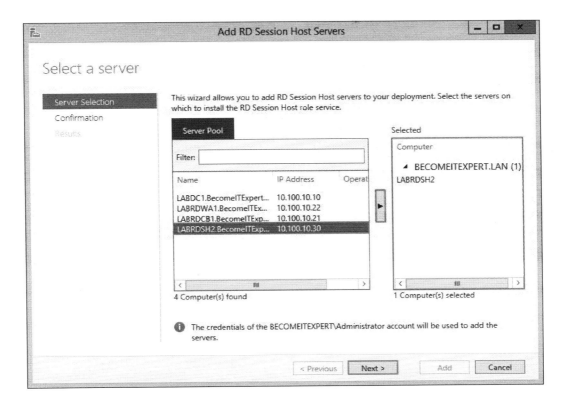

- Tick the "**Restart remote computers as needed**" box and click "**Add**":

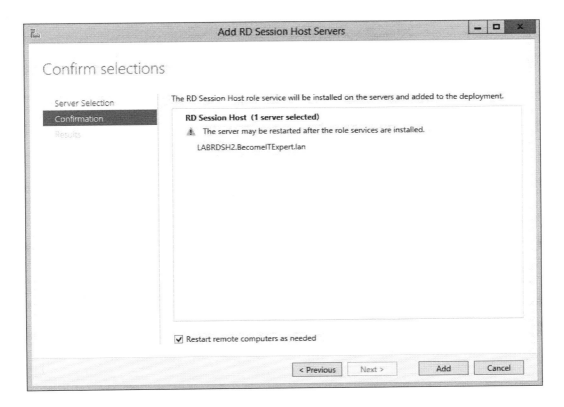

- Finally click "**Close**" to close the Wizard:

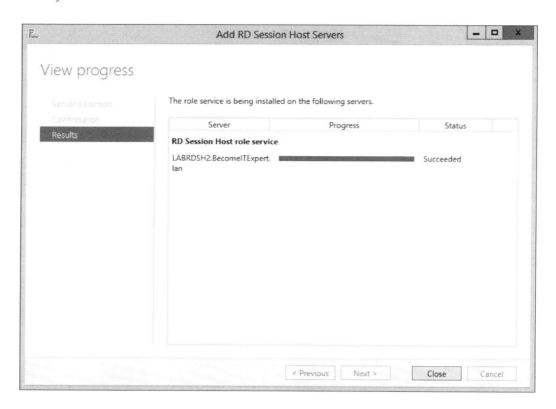

- Under "**DEPLOYMENT OVERVIEW**," right-click on "**RD Session Host**" and select "**Create Session Collection**":

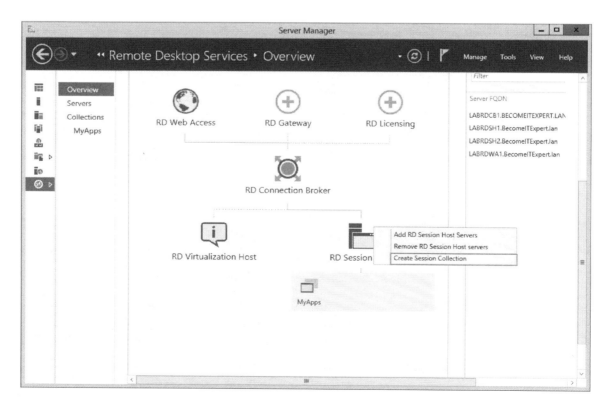

- Enter a Collection name and Description and then click "**Next**":

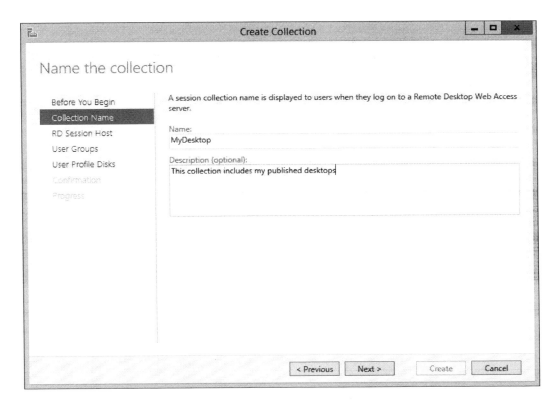

- Select and add the RDSH server "**LABRDSH2**" and click "**Next**" :

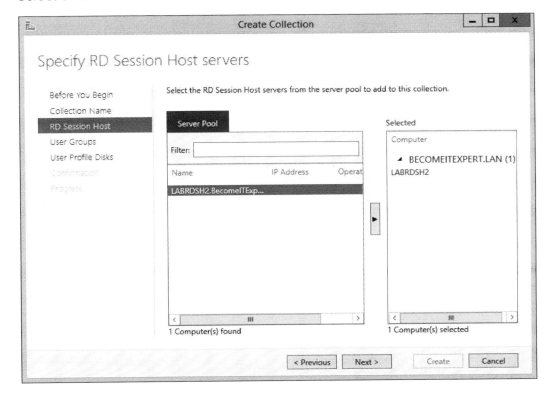

- You can create a dedicated AD security group and give it the access right to connect to this collection, in the following example, an AD security group named "**RDSDesktopUsers**" was created and will be specified at this new Windows Desktop Collection:

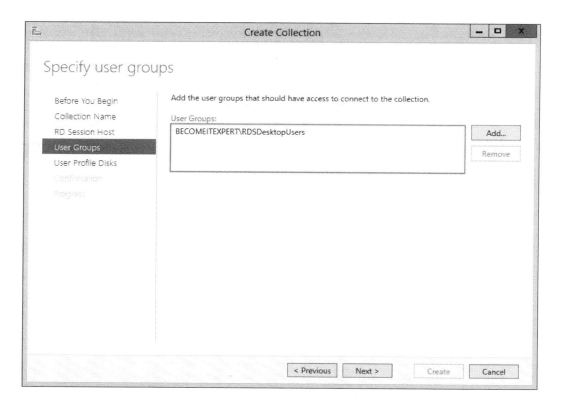

- <u>Do not enable</u> the user profile disks option and click "**Next**":

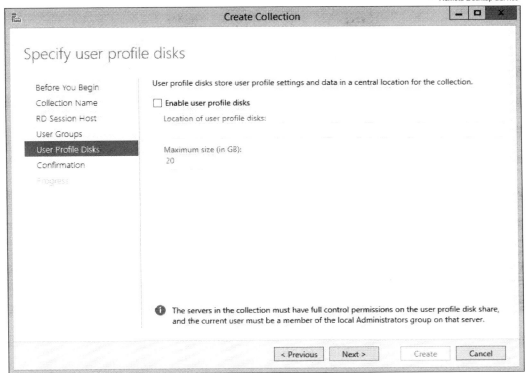

- Confirm the informations and click "**Create**":

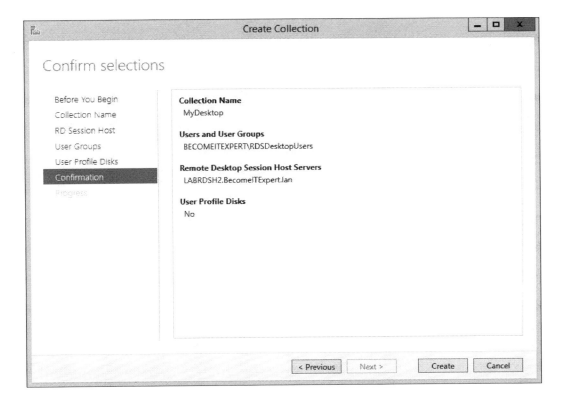

- Finally, click "**Close**" to exit the Wizard

- Open a Windows session on "LABW81" and connect to the RD Web Access portal using a user account member of the AD security group "**RDSDesktopUsers**". You can now see your published LABRDSH2 Windows Desktop:

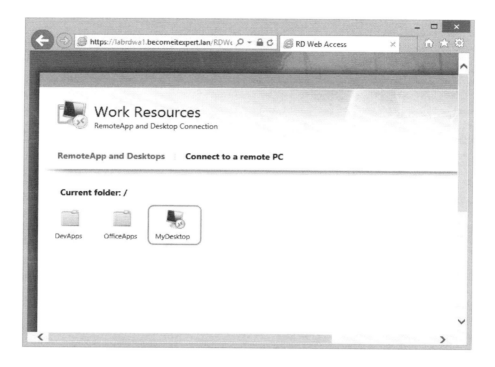

- Click on "**MyDesktop**" to start the Remote Desktop Connection to RDSH2 server

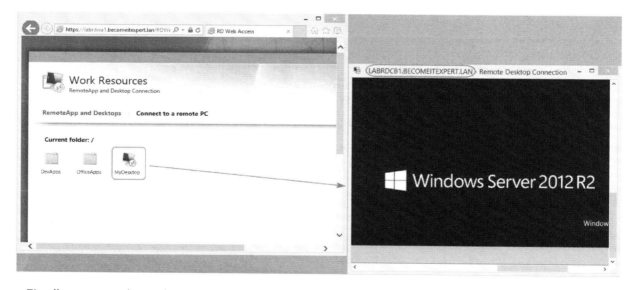

Finally, note that the Remote Desktop window displays the name of the RD Connection Broker server (or the name of the Broker Servers Farm if you're in HA mode) instead of the hostname of the remote RDSH server (LABRDSH2).

At this time, MyDesktop collection include only one RDSH Server (LABRDSH2), in a production environment, at least two RDSH Servers configured identically must be added to your Desktop Session Collection., the goal is to ensure Service Continuity.

Distribute your Windows Desktop

RemoteApp Programs distributions methods are applicable to Windows desktops, in fact Windows desktops can also be distributed via:

- RD Web Access Portal
- RDP Files (Manually copy RDP files Shortcuts):
  - Placed on the "Start Menu" or "Welcome Screen" on Windows 8 /8.1"
  - Placed on remote user's Windows Desktop
- The Modern "Remote Desktop" App available on Windows Store

As shown in the previous section, once published, Windows desktop appears on the RDWA Portal and has the same name as the collection to which it belongs.

Regarding the distribution of Windows desktops as RDP files, this can be done via the Control Panel, in our case, simply update the list of published resources to retrieve the Windows Desktop (LABRDSH2) we published previously

We will in the following example, refresh the "**RemoteApp and Desktop Connections**" tool to get our published Windows Desktop:

- Launch the "**RemoteApp and Desktop Connections**" tool from the Control Panel and click "**View details**":

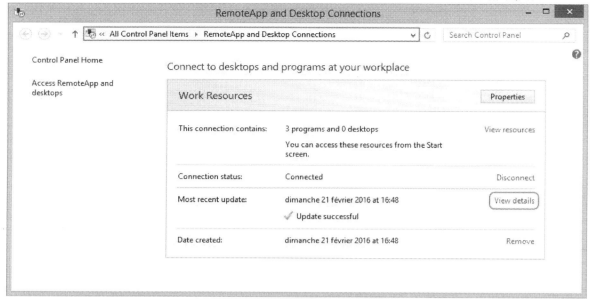

- Now, click on "**Update now**" :

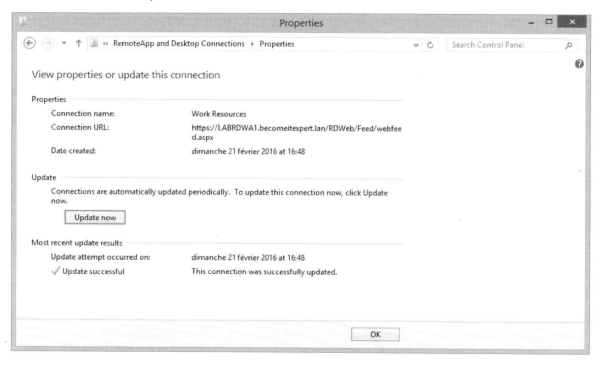

- The list of published resources is updated and our Windows desktop is now available:

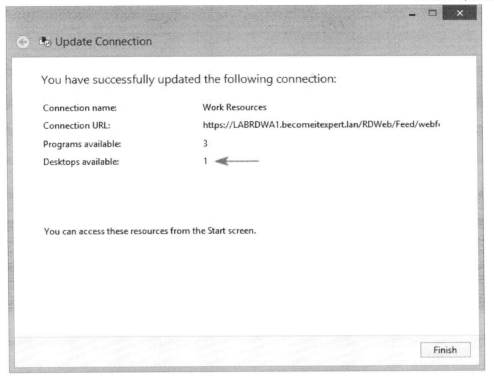

- This list is also updated in the Welcome screen of our LABW81 client:

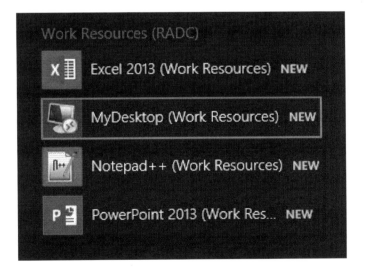

- The RDP file corresponding to our published Windows Desktop is also placed in the folder: C:\Users\%UserProfile%\AppData\Roaming\Microsoft\Windows\Start Menu\Programs\Work Resources (RADC)\

Finally, the update of the available resources on "Remote Desktop" App is done the same way as the "**RemoteApp and Desktop Connections**" tool, simply refresh the application to retrieve the new Windows desktop previously published.

Chapter 6. Manage your RDS 2012 R2 infrastructure

Managing an RDS infrastructure is often the concern of any IT in charge of the daily management and administration of this platform

In this chapter, we will discuss and discover all graphical and command-line management tools you have to know to correctly manage your RDS 2012 R2 infrastructure.

Management tools you need to know

RDS 2012 R2 platform can be managed via various graphical tools and command-line utilities, however the main RDS management tool is the Server Manager (**RDMS: R**emote **D**esktop **M**anagement **S**ervices), it allows to perform the following tasks:

- Add or remove RD servers to the deployment:
  - RD Session Host
  - RD Web Access
  - RD Gateway
  - RD Connection Broker
  - RD License Server
  - RD Virtualization Host
- Edit Deployment Properties
- Create, manage and delete Session & Virtualization Collections
- Edit Collections Properties
- Publish or unpublish RemoteApps Programs
- Edit RemoteApp Programs properties
- View event logs related to RDS
- Monitor RDS Windows Services
- Start RDS BPA (Best Practice Analyzer) to check the RDS role's health
- Configure performance alerts related to RDS role
- List all RDS servers
- View and manage Remote Desktop Sessions at a specific time :
  - Send a message to the remote user
  - Disconnect the Session of the remote user
  - End the Session of the remote user
  - Take control of the remote user's Session
- Allow or deny all remote desktop connections on a RDSH Server:
  - Enable or disable "Drain Mode"

Other RDS management tools exist:

- **RD Licensing Diagnoser tool** [installed by default with the RDSH server]: provides informations to help identify licensing issues for the Remote Desktop Session Host server (installed RDS CAL ...)
- **RD Gateway Manager tool** [installed by default with the RDG server]: this tool is used to create and manage Connection and Resource Authorization policies (CAP & RAP policies) for external RD users to internal published resources.

Finally, if you need to manage a large and complex RDS 2012 R2 infrastructure, there are several command-line tools like TSDiscon.exe, MSG.exe, and Logoff.exe ... that can be used.

In addition, a PowerShell Module (RemoteDesktop) is available and provided with RDS Windows Server 2012 and 2012 R2. It includes more than 70 RDS Cmd-Lets.

These command-line tools and PowerShell Cmd-lets allow you to perform the most deployment and management operations you can perform from the Server Manager.

The advantage of using CLI tools is the ability to create a powerful scripts and automate any repetitive, tedious and daily management tasks.

GUI Management Tools

Server Manager

With Windows Server 2012 and 2012 R2, the main management console for RDS is the Server Manager (RDMS). Indeed, after deployment of RDS role (whatever the deployment mode) a new Server Manager integrated-console appears in the left pane: **Remote Desktop Services**

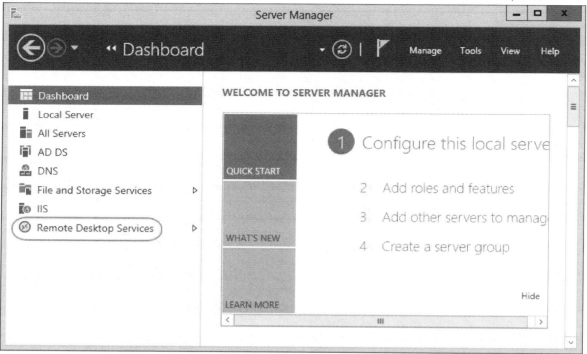

However, to manage your RDS infrastructure, you must gather all the RD servers deployed in the same management console (same server pool). In the following example, the Server Manager is launched from LABRDSH1 server, currently no other deployment server has been added and the following message is displayed from the "**Remote Desktop Services**" console:

 In RDS "Quick deployment mode", you do not need to add servers in the server pool as the three RDS role services are installed on the same server.

However, in a Standard RDS deployment (our case), RDS role services are installed on different servers, in that case they must be added to the Servers pool on the server from which the RDS infrastructure will be managed.

In the following example, all our RDS infrastructure will be managed from the DC "**LABDC1**" so:

- Go to the LABDC1 and open a Server Manager, then right-click on "**All servers**" and then select "**Add Servers**"

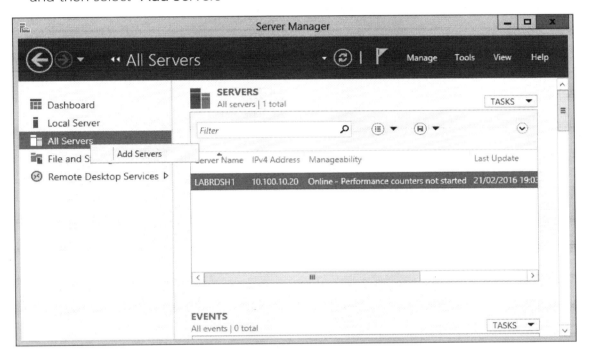

- **Search and select** all our RD Servers (for now: LABRDSH1 - LABRDCB1 LABRDWA1), then click the **right arrow** to add them and click OK

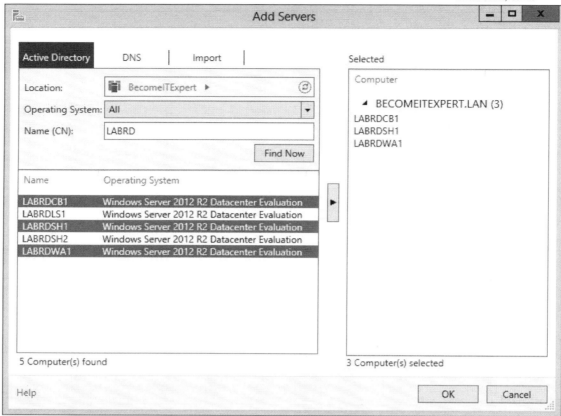

- The RD Servers added to the Server pool now appear under "**All servers**"

You can now manage your RDS infrastructure from the DC (from the Server Manager)

The screenshots below show all the features and configurations settings available on RDMS console.

- From the "**Overview**" pane, you have a quick start area that allows you to add RDSH servers and create new Sessions Collections.

 The buttons that allow you to add RDVH Servers and create Virtual Desktop Collections are greyed out because the RDVH role service is not installed.

- The "**Overview**" pane also contains a useful informations about the RDS deployment such as a complete list (with FQDN) of the RDS deployment servers.
  In addition "**DEPLOYMENT OVERVIEW**" section offers a visual presentation of the RDS architecture.
  By right-clicking the icon of RDWA, RDCB, or RDSH, an IT administrator can install additional RD servers or remove an existing servers. In other words, the architecture can expand as business needs.

  Finally, the (**+**) button allow to quickly deploy an RD Gateway or RD licensing servers and add them to the RDS deployment.

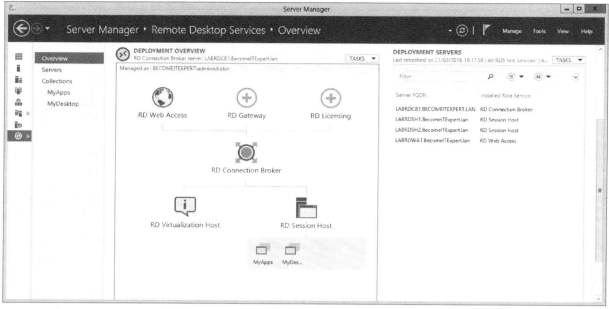

- The "**Servers**" pane contains all informations related to the RDS deployment servers including hostnames, IP addresses, their status "**Online/Offline**," the event logs of each RD server ...etc

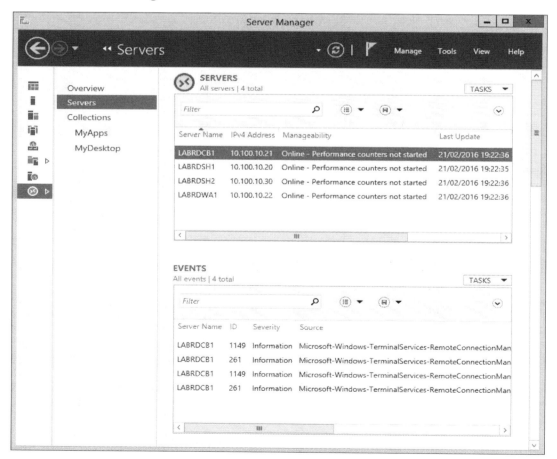

- The "**Servers**" pane also includes informations about Windows Services related to different RDS roles services, a performance counter that can be configured to

notify you of any performance issue and finally a **BPA** (**B**est **P**ractice **A**nalyzer) that collects detailed information on your RDS infrastructure health:

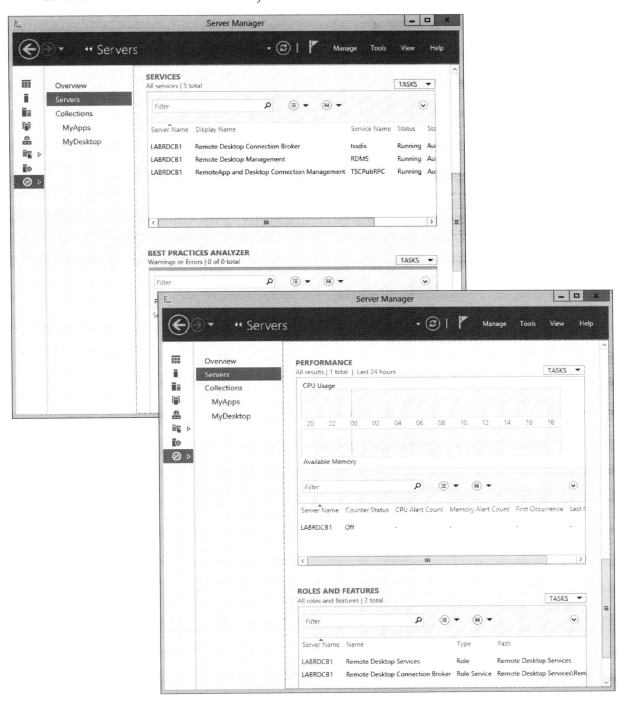

- The "**Collections**" pane allows you to view, create and delete RDS Collections, Edit your RDS deployment properties and also view the list of the RD Session Host servers of the deployment and Remote Desktop Connections with their status : Active /Disconneted

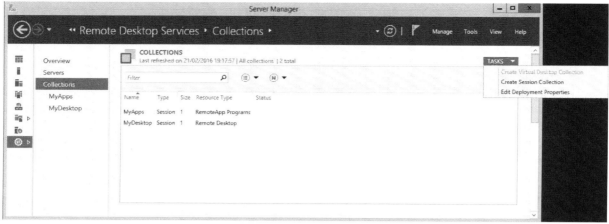

- Overview, Servers, Collections are a default panes available with your RDS deployment, other sub-pane are available when creating a new Session Collection. In our case, two Session Collections are created: "**MyApps**" and "**MyDesktop**". As shown below, two sub-panes with the same name of the RDS Session Collections are displayed:

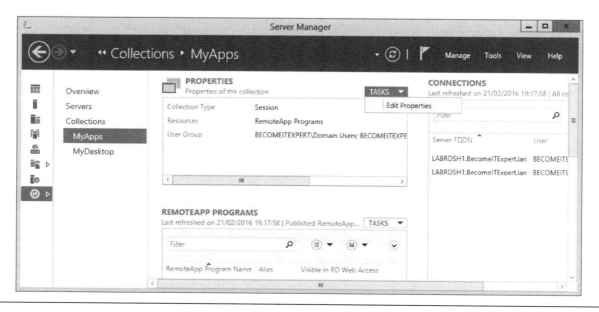

- The "**MyApps**" sub-pane allows you to publish or unpublish RemoteApp programs. You can also right-click on a RemoteApp program and edit its properties :

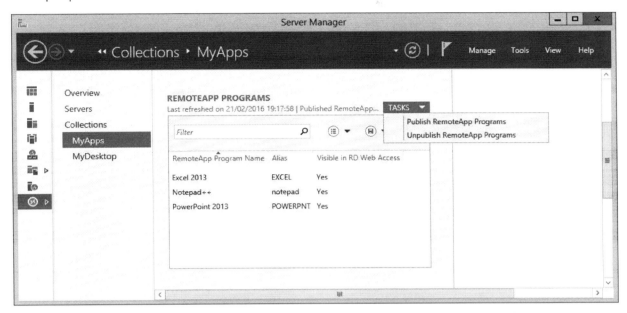

- Finally, the last section of this sub-pane (HOST SERVERS) contains the list of all RDSH servers being part of the Collection. You might want to prevent new user sessions from being created on one or more RDSH servers, this can be performed by right-clicking on it and selecting "**Do not allow new connections**." This can be useful if you have a planned maintenance on a RDSH server and want to make it unavailable temporarily:

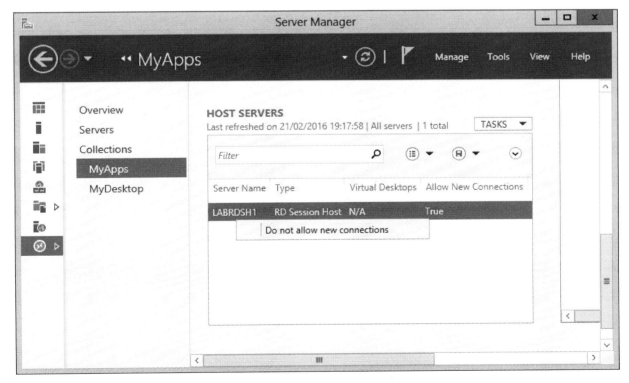

RD Licensing Diagnoser tool

After installing RDSH role service, a new RDS GUI tool named "RD Licensing Diagnoser tool" is automatically installed.

This tool collects and provides useful and important informations about your RDS licensing infrastructure: number of RDS CALs installed, License mode...

By default, it's placed in "**Administrative Tools**" folder, to launch it:

- Open a Windows session on LABRDSH1, from the "**Run**" menu, type "**Control AdminTools**":

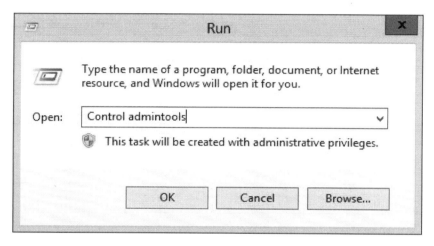

- Open "**Remote Desktop Services**" folder

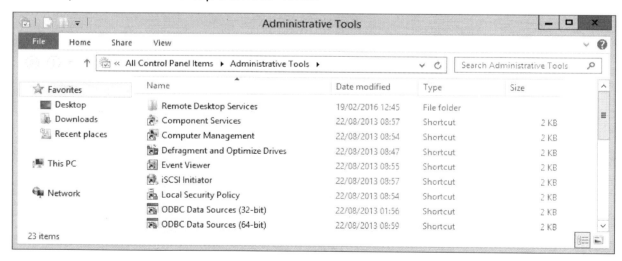

- Finally, double-click on "**RD Licensing Diagnoser**" tool to run it:

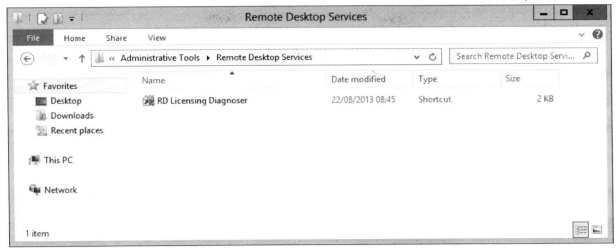

- The tool displays the collected informations such as the RDSH Server name and version, the number of RDS CALs available, RDS Licensing mode ...

 Two warnings related to the RDS licensing infrastructure are detected (The licensing mode is not configured & RDSH is within the grace period). We will fix these issues later in this book.

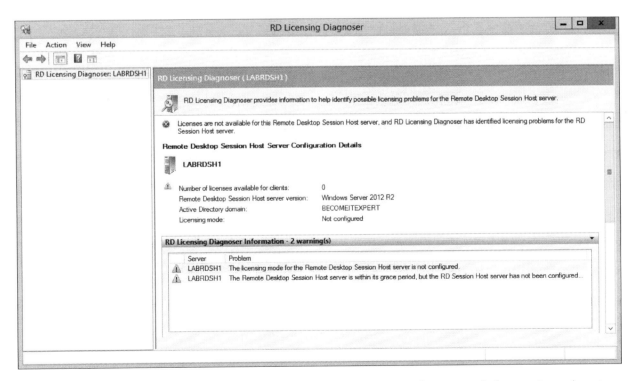

Refer to **Chapter 8. Licensing Remote Desktop Services** for more information about deploying and configuring the RDS Licensing infrastructure.

CLI Management Tools

Windows CLI tools

Several Command-line tools are provided with Windows 8.1 and Windows Server 2012 R2. These Command line tools allow you to perform the same tasks you can perform using Server Manager but also automate another tasks that can't be done via GUI tools such as:

- List all Process started by a user
- List Remote Sessions on a particular RemoteApp /RDSH Server
- Send a message to multiple remote users
- List of RDSH servers that have over 50 or 100 Active Sessions

The table below lists the most important and useful RDS CLI tools you need to know:

Nom de l'outil	Description
MSG.exe	Send a message to remote users
Logoff.exe	Close a remote desktop session
TSCon.exe	Link user session to a remote Session
TSDiscon.exe	Disconnect a remote desktop Session
Reset.exe	Reset a remote desktop Session
Query.exe	List Session (remote and local), Process, Users (remote and local)
Change.exe	Change RDSH Mode: installation – Execution
Chglogon.exe	Enable or Disable Remote Desktop Session

The syntax of the various Command line tools listed above is similar, just launch the Command Prompt (cmd.exe) or Windows PowerShell and type the tool name followed by /? Parameter to learn more.

In the following example, we will use MSG.exe tool for sending messages to a remote user (username: hkadiri) connected to LABRDSH1 server:

- Create an AD user account with the following information:
  - First Name : Your First Name
  - Last Name : Your Last Name
  - Username : initial of the first name and Last Name (ex: hkadiri for Hicham KADIRI)
  - Password: Specify a password for your user account
  - Add your user account to "RDSUsers" security group.

- Log In on the client "**LABW81**" and start a RemoteApp program or a Remote Desktop connection to MyDesktop Collection

- Now open a Windows Session on LABRDSH1 Server and run the Command Prompt (cmd.exe) or Windows PowerShell and type the following command to send a message to your remote user (hkadiri in the following example)

    o MSG hkadiri **"Hello, a maintenance is planned on this server at 2P.M. Please save your work and logoff your session ASAP | IT Team"**

 You can send a message to your user from a remote server by specifying /Server parameter, the command to use becomes: MSG UserName /Server:LABRDSH1 "Your message"

- The remote user receives your message that will be displayed on his remote session:

```
Message from administrator 6/21/2016 5:48 AM
Hello, a maintenance is planned on this server at 2P.M. Please save your work and logoff your session ASAP | IT Team
                                                                    OK
```

« RemoteDesktop » PowerShell Module

With Windows Server 2012 and 2012 R2, Microsoft has introduced a new PowerShell module named (**RemoteDesktop**), it includes more than 70 Cmd-lets that allow you to deploy, configure and manage your RDS infrastructure. The complete list of these Cmd-Let can obtained by using the following command:
Get-Command –Module RemoteDesktop

 "RemoteDesktop" Cmd-lets within Windows Server 2012 R2 now includes the "RD" extension. E.g **New-RDSessionDeployment** with RDS 2012 R2 instead of **New-SessionDeployment** with RDS 2012.

[PowerShell screenshot showing output of `Get-Command -Module RemoteDesktop` listing RDS cmdlets]

As explained earlier in this Book, this PowerShell module can be used to deploy RDS platform, create a Session collections and publish RemoteApp Programs.
It can also be used to manage the RDS infrastructure.

In the following example, we will use RemoteDesktop Module to:
- Get the list of all RDS servers of the deployment

"RemoteDesktop" Module must be imported before using its Cmdlets. To import this module, use the following command:
Import-Module RemoteDesktop

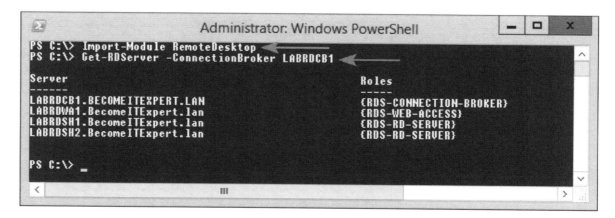

- Get the list of RemoteApp programs published on the "**MyApps**" Collection:

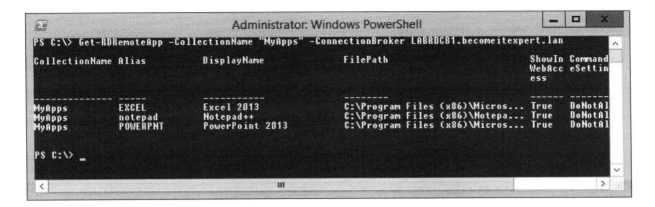

- Get the list of all active sessions hosted on the "**MyApps**" Session Collection:

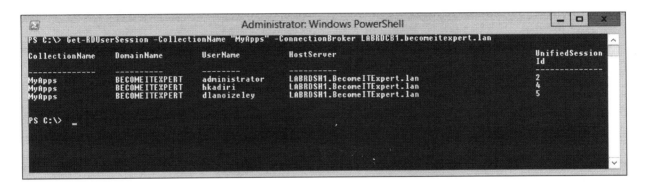

RDS Management via Scripts

Whereas in the past scripting was somewhat hard to do, required special installations of various implementations, and was rather limited in its effect, with the release of Microsoft Windows 8.1 and Windows Server 2012 R2, scripting is coming into its own.

This is really as it should be. However, most Administrators and IT professionals do not have an understanding of scripting, because in the past scripting was not a powerful alternative for platform management.

However, in a large enterprise, it is a vital reality that one simply cannot perform management from the GUI management tools because it is too time-constraining, too error prone, and after a while too irritating. Clearly there needs to be a better way, and there is.

Scripting is the answer

Batch and PowerShell Scripts based on the command-line tools and Cmd-lets described in the previous section can also be used to manage the RDS 2012 R2 infrastructure.

If you have to manage a large RDS infrastructure (dozens of RDS servers and hundreds or even thousands of remote desktop connections), you can automate all the management and administration tasks.

We will in the following example write a simple Batch script that allow you to send a message to one or more Remote Desktop users:

- Open Notepad and type the following code:

```
@Echo Off
Set /P RemoteUser= Enter a username or type * to send your message to everyone:
Set /P Message= Enter your message here:
MSG %RemoteUser% %Message%
Echo "Your message has been sent"
Pause
```

- Save the file as a Batch script (with .BAT or .CMD extensions)
- Run the script (as Administrator) and specify the required values

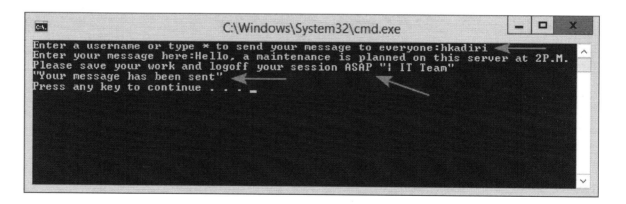

- As shown in the image above, the script was used to send a message to the user "hkadiri". After running the script and sending the message, the remote user receives the message on his remote session:

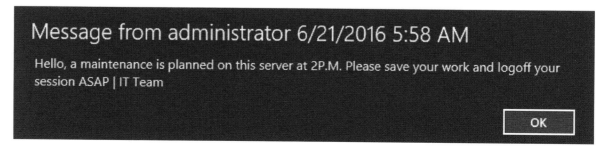

Chapter 7. Secure your RDS 2012 R2 Infrastructure

Obviously, potential security issues depend on how you deploy RDS. If you have a more complex setup, with users connecting over the Internet and/or via a web browser, you'll have more security issues to address than if you have a simple deployment where users only connect via the RDC client over the LAN.

RDS includes a number of security mechanisms to help you make RD connections more secure.

This chapter will discuss all security options related to RDS 2012 R2 and how to implement them.

Securing the RD User Environment

The following topics will be discussed in this section:

- Locking down the servers (and why you should do so)
- Optimizing the user experience
- Configuring remote control of a session
- Securing access to the RD Session Host server

Locking Down the RDSH Server

Whatever the type of resource published on a Session Collection (RemoteApp Program or Windows Desktop), a Remote Desktop user can open a remote Desktop Session on all RDSH servers being part of the Session Collection to which it has access.

Indeed, access to RemoteApp programs automatically give the right to open Remote Desktop Sessions.

Today, companies require a high level of security for their infrastructure, they do not accept that a simple RDS user can see and navigate between the different partitions and disks of the RDSH server.

As a RDS platform Administrator, you can set up and configure various security options to lock down your RDSH servers and highly secure the access to them.

By using Group Policy settings, you can restrict access to most options and components of your RDSH servers:

- Restricting Device and Resource Redirection
- Restricting Printers Redirection
- Restricting access to Control Panel

- Restricting the Printer Drivers Installation
- Restricting access to Registry
- Restricting access to Windows Automatic Updates
- Restricting access to the Start Menu and Network options
- Hide Desktop icons
- Restricting access to CD and Floppy Drive
- Restricting access to Command Prompt (CMD.exe)
- Restricting access to Task Manager

Refer to the instructions below for more informations.

Restricting Device and Resource Redirection

Restricting Device and Resource Redirection can be configured using the following Group Policy parameter:

- Computer Configuration | Policies | Administrative Templates | Windows Components | Remote Desktop Services | Session Host Remote Desktop | redirection of device and resource

Restricting Printers Redirection

Restricting Printers Redirection can be configured using the following Group Policy parameter:

- Computer Configuration | Policies | Administrative Templates | Windows Components | Remote Desktop Services | Session Host Remote Desktop | Printer Redirection

Restricting access to Control Panel

Restricting access to the Control Panel can be configured using the following Group Policy parameter:

- User Configuration | Policies | Administrative Templates | Control Panel
  - Parameter: Deny access to Control Panel and PC settings

Restricting the Printer Drivers Installation

Restricting the Printer Drivers installation can be configured using the following Group Policy parameter:

- Computer Configuration | Policies | Windows Settings | Security Settings | Local Policies | Security Options
    - Parameter : Devices: Prevent users from installing printer drivers

⇨ **Restricting access to Registry**

Restricting access to the Registry can be configured using the following Group Policy parameter:

- User Configuration | Policies | Administrative Templates | System
    - Parameter : Prevent access to registry editing tools

⇨ **Restricting access to Windows Automatic Updates**

Restricting access to Windows Updates can be configured using the following Group Policy parameter:

- User Configuration | Policies | Administrative Templates | System
    - Parameter : Windows Automatic Updates

⇨ **Restricting access to the Start Menu and Network options**

Restriction access to the Start Menu and Network options can be configured using the following Group Policy parameter:

- User Configuration | Policies | Administrative Templates | Started Menu and Taskbar
    - Parameter: disable the settings that match your needs!

⇨ **Hide Desktop icons**

Desktop icons can be hidden by using the following Group Policy parameters:

- User Configuration | Policies | Administrative Templates | Desktop
    - Parameters:
        - Hide and disable all items on the desktop
        - Delete "My Computer" from the Desktop

⇨ Restricting access to the CD and Floppy Drive

Restricting access to CD and Floppy can be configured using the following Group Policy parameters:

- Computer Configuration | Policies | Windows Settings | Security Settings | Local Policies | Security Options
    - Parameters:
        - Devices: Allow access to CD-ROM only to users who are locally logged on
        - Devices: Allow floppy drive access to local logged on user only

⇨ Restricting access to the Command Prompt

Restricting access to Command Prompt (cmd.exe) can be configured using the following Group Policy parameter:

- User Configuration | Policies | Administrative Templates | System
    - Parameter : Disable access to Command Prompt

⇨ Restricting access to Task Manager

Restricting access to the Task Manager can be configured using the following Group Policy parameter:

- User Configuration | Policies | Administrative Templates | System | Ctrl + Alt + Del Options
- Parameter:
    - Remove Task Manager

Prevent users from running unwanted applications

The goal is to prevent remote users from running any applications to which you have not granted access.

Preventing remote user from running Unwanted Apps can be configured by using the following Group Policy parameters:

- User Configuration | Policies | Administrative Templates | System
    - Parameters :
        - Do not run specified Windows applications
        - Run only specified Windows applications

 You can also use AppLocker feature that's provided with Windows Server 2012 R2 to set a specific "white-list" and block unauthorized applications, scripts, macros, or any other executables from running on your RD Session Host servers.

Keeping the RD Session Host Server Available
Allowing or Denying Access to the RD Session Host Server

Although users cannot log on to the RD Session Host server unless they are members of the local Remote Desktop Users group on that RD Session Host server, you can control the ability of users to log by using the following Group Policy parameter:

- o Computer Configuration | Policies | Administrative Templates | Windows Components | Remote Desktop Services | Remote Desktop Session Host | Connections | Allow Users To Connect Remotely Using Remote Desktop Services

This setting controls whether users can access the RD Session Host server remotely.

An RD Session Host server will not accept any user logons until the Remote Desktop Users group is populated.

This policy gives you more detailed control over who has access to the RD Session Host servers so that you can prevent unauthorized users from consuming licenses that you had intended for people who need them.

 It's also possible to prevent logons to the RD Session Host server via Active Directory Users and Computers; one option in the user account Properties dialog box defines whether users are allowed to log on to the RD Session Host server (they are, by default). Although it might appear that Group Policy or Active Directory Users and Computers settings are good ways to prevent people from logging on during server maintenance, they're really not, because the policy might not apply in time and you might not have Active Directory Domain Services (AD DS) control anyway. To lock out users during maintenance, run the following command on the RD Session Host that you need to work on: **Change Logon /Disable**

Limiting the Number of RD Session Host Server Connections

For application licensing reasons or performance reasons, you might want to limit the number of simultaneous connections to the RDSH server. Do this with the following GPO setting:

- o Computer Configuration | Policies | Administrative Templates | Windows Components | Remote Desktop Services | Remote Desktop Session Host | Connections | Limit Number of Connections

Enable the Limit Number of Connections setting to limit the total number of simultaneous connections that can be active on an RD Session Host server. If you have 100 users, and each user is limited to one session, you know that you can limit the number of connections to approximately 100 and not interfere with user access.

This also ensures that you won't allow more connections than are needed

Setting Session Time Limits

The GPOs to set time limits on active, idle, and disconnected sessions are located at:

- o Computer Configuration | Policies | Administrative Templates | Windows Components | Remote Desktop Services | Remote Desktop Session Host | Session Time Limits

RD Session Host Drain Mode

RDSH Drain Mode prevents new users from logging onto the server, while allowing currently logged on users to reconnect to their existing sessions. By waiting for existing users to save their work and log off, the administrator can take a RDSH server down for maintenance without causing user data loss.

There are two ways an administrator can put a RDSH server into drain mode:

- Using the command-line tool : Chglogon.exe (or CHANGE.exe logon)
- Using RDMS UI : Server Manager

The command-line tool chglogon.exe (or "change logon") may be used to configure the drain mode. There are five options: /QUERY, /ENABLE, /DISABLE, /DRAIN, /DRAINUNTILRESTART

- **ENABLE**: enables logons from client sessions, but not from the console.
- **DISABLE**: disables subsequent logons from client sessions, but not from the console. Does not affect currently logged on users.

- **DRAIN** [MAINTENANCE MODE]: disables logons from new client sessions, but allows reconnections to existing sessions.
- **DRAINUNTILRESTART** [MAINTENANCE MODE]: disables logons from new client sessions until the computer is restarted, but allows reconnections to existing sessions.

To learn more, consult the following link:
https://technet.microsoft.com/en-us/library/cc753586(v=ws.11).aspx

By default, RDSH Servers are set to "ENABLE mode"
Note that the Server Manager allows you to put RDSH servers in "ENABLE & DRAIN" mode only.

To put RDSH servers in one of the 4 modes listed above, you must use ChgLogon.exe command line tool.

HowTo : put RDSH server in "DRAIN mode" using Server Manager

We are going in the following example to put LABRDSH1 server in DRAIN mode:

- Open a Windows session on DC "LABDC1"
- Launch the Server Manager and click "Remote Desktop Services"
- From the left pane, Select "MyApps" Collection
- Under "**HOST SERVERS**", right-click on LABRDSH1 server and select " **Do not allow new connections** ":

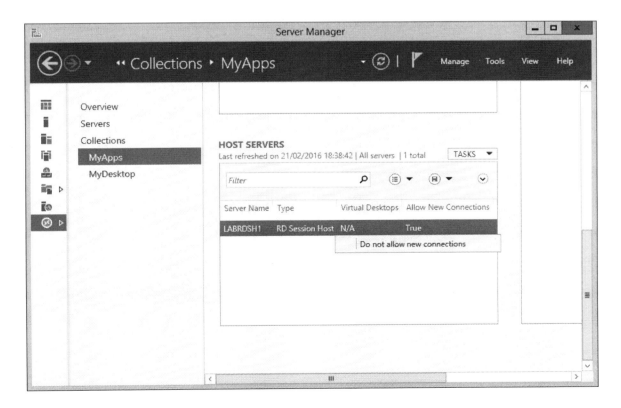

- LABRDSH1 server is now in Drain mode
- If you try to start a new remote desktop connection, the following message is displayed

▷ **HowTo : put RDSH server in "DRAIN mode" using Chglogon.exe tool**
- Open a Windows session on the RDSH server you want to put in Drain Mode (LABRDSH2 in the following example)
- Run the Command Prompt (cmd.exe) or Windows PowerShell as administrator and type: **Change Logon /Drain**

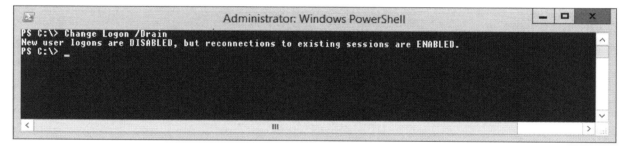

- To put LABRDSH2 in "ENABLE mode", use the following command:
Change Logon /Enable

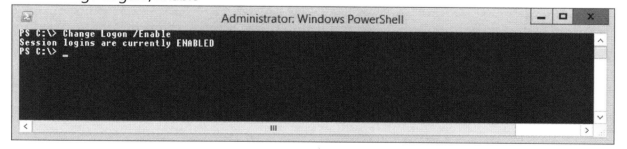

If you have to restart the RDSH server after the maintenance, it is recommended to put the server in "**DRAINUNTILRESTART mode"**, this can be done by using the following command:
Change Logon /DRAINUNTILRESTART

Taking Remote Control of User Sessions: RDS Shadowing

Microsoft has brought Remote Desktop Shadowing to Windows Server 2012 R2 and Windows 8.1. We remind that Shadow mode (Shadow session) can be used by administrator to view and manage any active remote user session. This mode has been supported almost since the first Microsoft Terminal Server versions and was suddenly removed from Windows Server 2012 (due to the transfer of the stack rdp from kernel to user mode).

RDS Shadow can be used from two tools:

- Server Manager
- MSTSC.exe Tool

➪ RDS Shadow from the Server Manager

The shadow UI is located in Server Manager under Remote Desktop Services > Collections.

- Start a RemoteApp Program or open a Remote Desktop Session. This will create an Active session on your RDSH server that host the RemoteApp Program.
- Start the Server Manager and click "**Remote Desktop Services**"
- Select "**MyApps**" Collection
- All active sessions hosted on the "**MyApps**" Collection are displayed under "**CONNECTIONS**"
- Simply right-click a user's session and choose "**Shadow**" from the context menu, then choose "**View**" option (Screen Sharing only) or control (Take Remote Control) the session with or without consent.
    - o _Note:_ *We are going first to view the remote session*

- A Remote Monitoring Request appears on the remote user's Session:

- Once remote user accepts the Request, its remote session is shared with the Administrator:

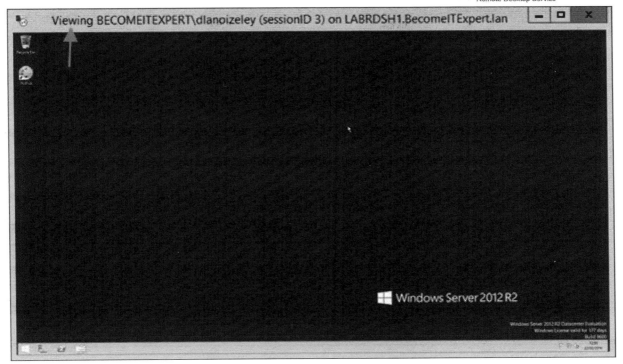

- If you select "Control", a new Remote Control Request is sent to remote user and the following notification is displayed:

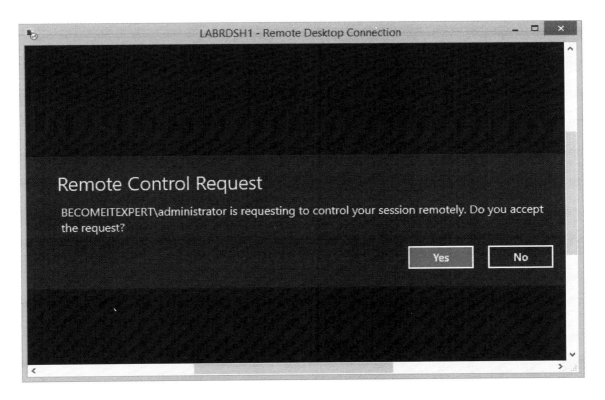

- Once accepted, you can take control of its session and make changes in order to troubleshoot and resolve a potential problem encountered on a program, applications, ...:

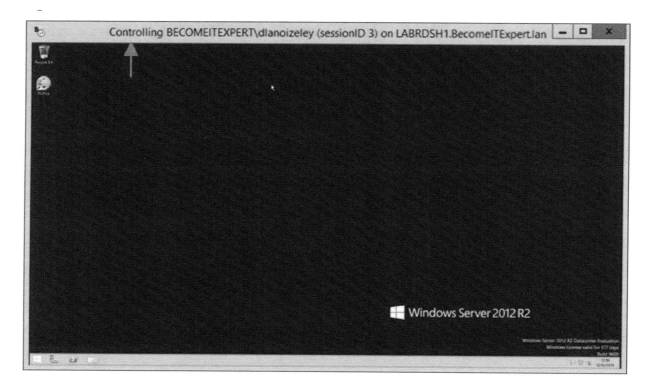

⇨ RDS Shadow from MSTSC.exe command line tool

The MSTSC command line tool can also be used to view and control remote desktop sessions.

Note that you must first collect informations about the remote session and at least know its ID to be able to view or control it via MSTSC.exe tool, to do this:

- Run the Command Prompt (cmd.exe) or Windows PowerShell as administrator and enter the following command to list the active sessions on a specific RDSH server (LABRDSH1 in the following example):
  QUERY SESSION /Server:LABRDSH1

- As shown in the image below, "dlanoizeley" user's session ID is 3, to view this remote session, run the following command by specifying the RDSH server that hosts that session:
  MSTSC /V:LABRDSH1 /Shadow:3

  To control the remote session, /Control parameter must be specified after the /shadow option, the command will therefore be:
  MSTSC /V:LABRDSH1 /Shadow:3 /Control

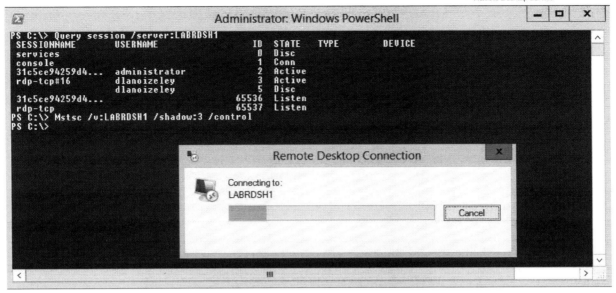

Securing RDP Connections

This chapter explains the Key RDS communication security features and supporting technologies.

Core Security Features and Technologies

The figure below shows the features that will be discussed and the technologies supporting each feature

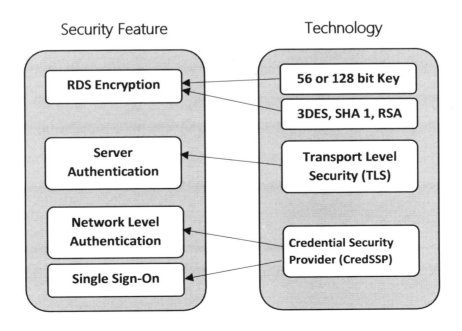

Authenticating RDSH Server Identity (Server Authentication)

One danger of communicating with a remote computer that requires you to supply your credentials is that the server might not be what you think it is. If it's a rogue server impersonating a real one, you could inadvertent type your credentials into the wrong server, thereby giving attackers everything that they need to connect to your domain or server.

RDP includes encryption, but the protocol does not have any means to authenticate the server.

That's where TLS and CredSSP come in Domain users and individual servers can be authenticated with Kerberos on the Local Area Network (LAN) Server farms by default can't because the farm has no identity in Active Directory Domain Services (AD DS) for the Kerberos ticket to look up.

For LAN scenarios, you can use Kerberos to authenticate to the farm.

To authenticate to a farm or servers over the Internet, you will use TLS rather than Kerberos

How can i set SSL (TLS) security layer for my RDS deployment?

To define the security layer to "SSL (TLS 1.0)", edit the properties of your Session Collection, click on "**Security**" pane and then select "**SSL (TLS 1.0)**" under "**Security Layer**":

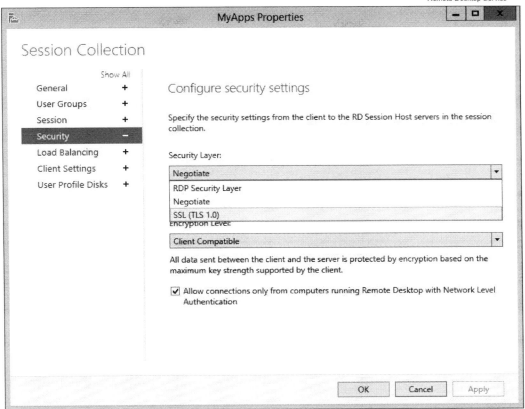

This setting can also be configured via GPO:

Computer Configuration | Policies | Administrative Templates | Windows Components | Remote Desktop Services | Remote Desktop Session Host | Security

Parameter: **Require use of specific layer for remote (RDP) connections**

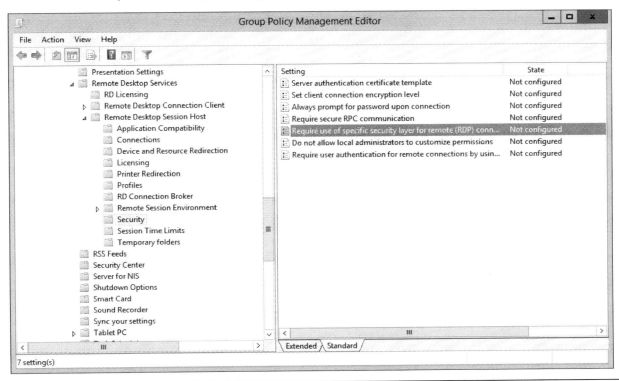

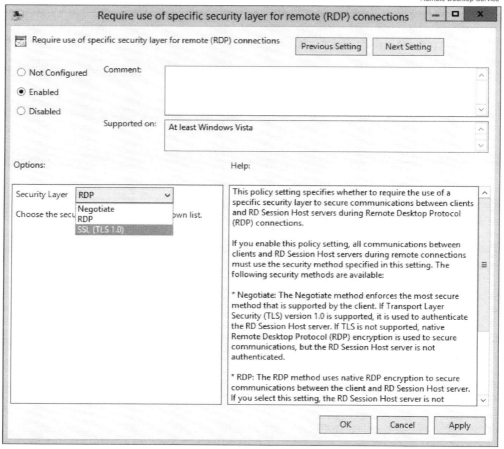

Encrypting RDP Data /Traffic

RDP clients support three levels of encryption: Low, High, and FIPS-compliant.

Low security uses only a 56-bit key to encrypt traffic and will not support server authentication.
It also encrypts only traffic going from client to server, not that going from server to client.

High security uses a 128-bit key to encrypt data going between client and server; it encrypts traffic going in both directions.
You can use High security to support TLS-based server authentication.

FIPS-compliant security uses FIPS-compliant algorithms for encrypting the data flow between the client and the server.
Federal Information Processing Standard (**FIPS**) describes the standards for key generation and key management. There's no such thing as FIPS encryption, but many encryption mechanisms are FIPS-compliant. Only algorithms submitted to the

National Institute of Standards and Technology (NIST) can be considered FIPS-compliant.
FIPS-compliant security supports server authentication for RDP connections

How can i encrypt RDP traffic?

Simply edit the properties of your Session Collection, click on "**Security**" pane and under "**Encryption level**" select:

- **High**: if your network machines are running Windows 7 /2008 R2 or higher
- **Client Compatible**: if your network machines are running Windows XP /2003

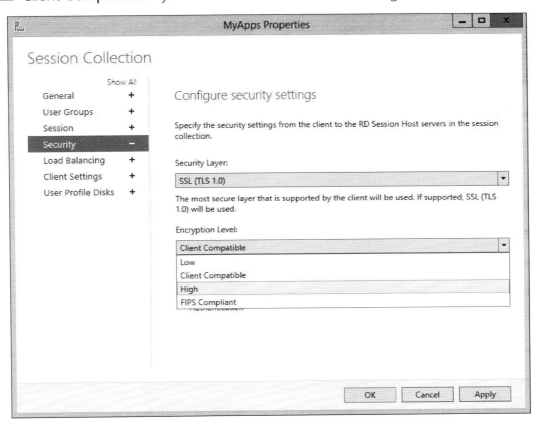

This setting can also be configured via GPO:

Computer Configuration | Policies | Administrative Templates | Windows Components | Remote Desktop Services | Remote Desktop Session Host | Security

Parameter: **Set client connection encryption level**

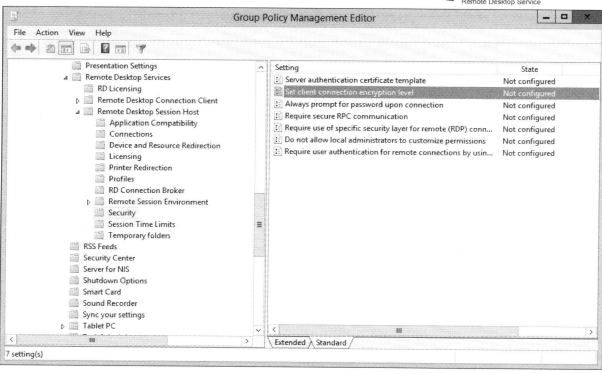

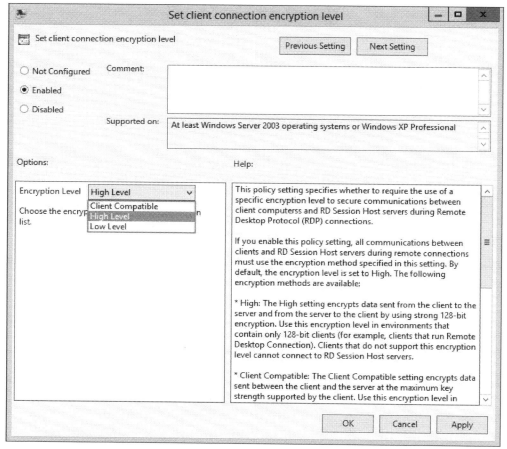

Authenticating Client Identity with Network Level Authentication (NLA)

Authenticating the server protects the client from connecting to a malicious RD Session Host server masquerading as a legitimate one, but what about protecting the RD Session Host server from malicious connections?

The process of starting a connection—even just presenting a logon screen—requires the server to create many of the processes required to support a session (for example, Csrss.exe and Winlogon.exe).

Session creation is expensive, so creating even this much of a session—only to be told that the user trying to access the RD Session Host server doesn't have the required credentials—is both a security vulnerability and a performance hit.

One way to reduce both the security hit and the performance hit is to enable connections only from computers that support **NLA** (**N**etwork **L**evel **A**uthentication).

NLA uses CredSSP to present user credentials to the server before the server has to create a session.

You might have noticed that when you connect to an RD Session Host server with the RDC 6x or later client, you don't connect to the RD Session Host server logon screen to provide your credentials. Instead, a local dialog box pops up to take your credentials on the client. This dialog box is the front end of CredSSP

Note that the NLA is enabled by default on any newly created Session Collection.

Edit the properties of your Session Collection, click on "**Security**" pane and confirm that "**Allow connections only from computers ..... with Network Level Authentication**" option is ticked:

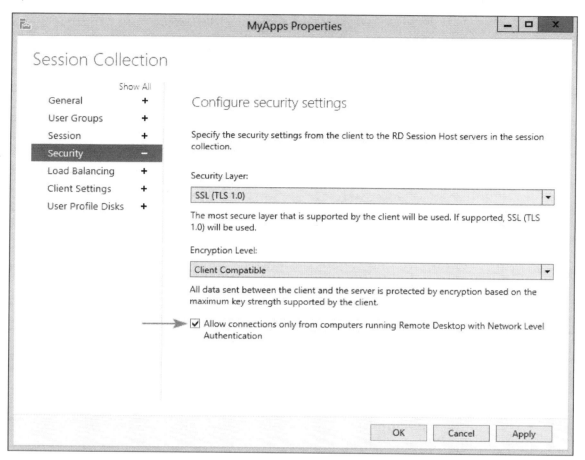

This setting can also be configured via GPO:

Computer Configuration | Policies | Administrative Templates | Windows Components | Remote Desktop Services | Remote Desktop Session Host | Security

Parameter: **Require user authentication for remote connections by using Network Level Authentication**

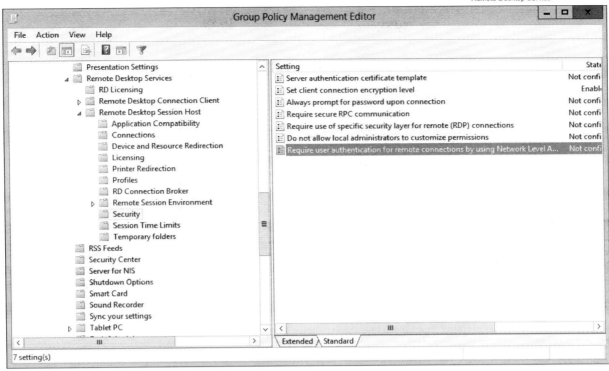

Chapter 8. Licensing Remote Desktop Services

Once deployed, Remote Desktop Services (RDS) role works only for a limited time (120 days) without licensing.

During the evaluation period, you can test and validate the RDS Solution and its features to decide if it meets your needs.

After the evaluation period has elapsed, at least one RD Licensing server must be installed and configured on your RDS deployment.

RDS Licensing Model

There are two RDS licensing model with Windows Server 2012 R2:

- **RDS Licensing** (RDS CAL : RDS Client Access License)
  - Licensing to access RD Session Host sessions (including VMs) and to use other RDS role services (such as RD Gateway, RD Connection Broker, and RD Web Access)
- **VDI Licensing** (VDI CAL : VDI Client Access License)
  - Licensing to access pooled or personal VMs hosted on the RD Virtualization Host server and to use RD Connection Broker. This licensing mode is intended for people who need only Virtual Desktop Infrastructure (VDI) and don't need other RDS role services (for example, RD Gateway for WAN access)

Only one Licensing model was available with Windows Server 2000/ 2003 /2008: **TS CALs** (Terminal Services Client Access Licenses)

RDS Licensing

RDS CALs give users or devices the right to access and use any of the RDS role services. This is why RDS CALs are part of the requirements for VDI access.

There are four RDS licensing options to choose from, and which option you choose depends on how your company operates.

The four RDS licensing options are:

- **Per-User Licensing**: each user that will use RDS role service(s) needs to have an RDS User CAL. Purchase RDS User CALs when your users will access RDS role service(s) from multiple machines. This mode allows users to access RDS resources from any computer because the license is limited to the user, not the device. RDS Device CALs, conversely, are limited to the accessing device.

- **Per-Device Licensing**: each device that will use RDS role service(s) needs to have an RDS Device CAL. Purchase RDS Device CALs when multiple users will access RDS role service(s) from a set number of client devices. A good example of when RDS Device CALs are the better choice is shift work—when multiple users at different times of the day will use one machine to access RDS resources. RDS Device CALs are also required to access pooled or personal VMs

- **RDS External Connector**: this license option allows multiple external users (users who are not part of your company and for whom you do not provide licensing) to access one specific server.
  Each server accessed would need a license, for example, if you were going to license access to an RD Session Host server on one server, via RD Gateway on another server, you would need a license for both servers

- **Services Provider License Agreement (SPLA)**: this licensing is specifically for hosting providers and independent service vendors (ISVs) that host RDS and provide RDS access rights as part of their offering

Of the four options, RDS (Per-User or Per-Device) CALs are most commonly used with RDS. RD Session Host servers can be configured only in Per-User or Per-Device mode, but not both. Most people purchase one type of RDS CAL.
You might use both if providing both VMs and sessions: Per-User CALs to access RD Session Host servers and RDS Per-Device CALs to use pooled and personal VMs

TS CALs 2008 and RDS CALs 2008 R2 can be reinstalled and reused on a License Server for RDS 2012 and 2012 R2.

Note that only one Licensing option was available with Windows Server 2000: **Per-Device**. On Windows Server 2003 /2008 /2008 R2 two licensing options were available: **Per-User & Per-Device**

License Tracking and Enforcement

Some RDS license options are enforced while others are not. The same is true for tracking license allocation.

The table below shows which licenses are tracked, enforced, both, or neither

RDS License type	Tracked	Enforced
RDS User CAL	✓	✗
RDS Device CAL	✓	✓
External Connector Licenses	✗	✗

Per-User licensing is tracked but not enforced, whereas Per-Device licensing is tracked and enforced, this does not mean that you are not bound by your license agreement, however—you are required to purchase the proper amount of licenses for your environment whether or not the licensing mode is enforced.

You can have up to two concurrent administrative connections to an RD Session Host server for administrative purposes. Administrative connections do not require an RDS CAL.

Installing RD License Server

During this section, we are going to deploy our first RD License server.

RDLS role service will be deployed on a dedicated server named "**LABRDSL1** ".

Note that this server (VM) has already been deployed and joined to the AD domain.

Follow the instructions below to successfully deploy the RD License Server:

- Open a Windows session on the DC "**LABDC1** " and launch the Server Manager
- Add the server "**LABRDLS1**" to the Servers Pool (All Servers pane):

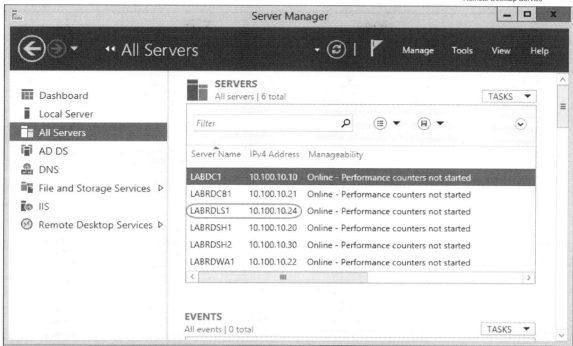

- Under "**Remote Desktop Services**" and "**DEPLOYMENT OVERVIEW**", click on the "**RD Licensing**" + button:

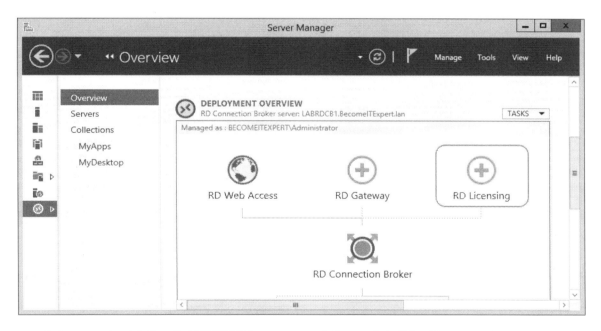

- Select and add the "**LABRDLS1**" server and then click "**Next**" to continue:

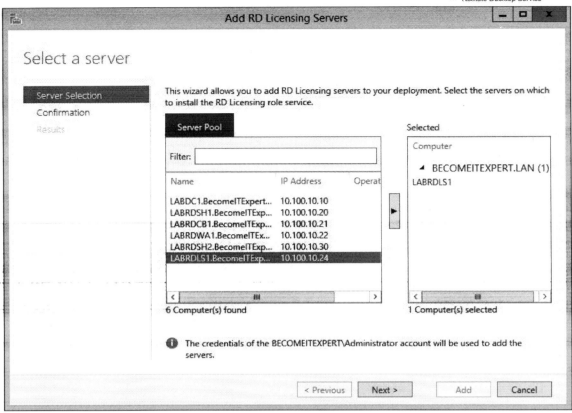

- Click on "**Add** " to add LABRDLS1 server to the deployment:

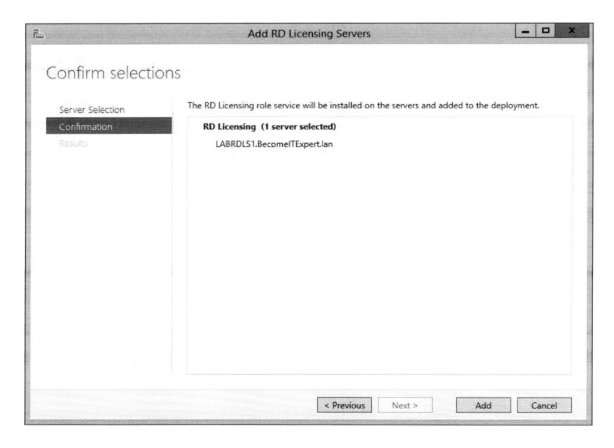

- Once added, click on "**Close**" to exit the Wizard:

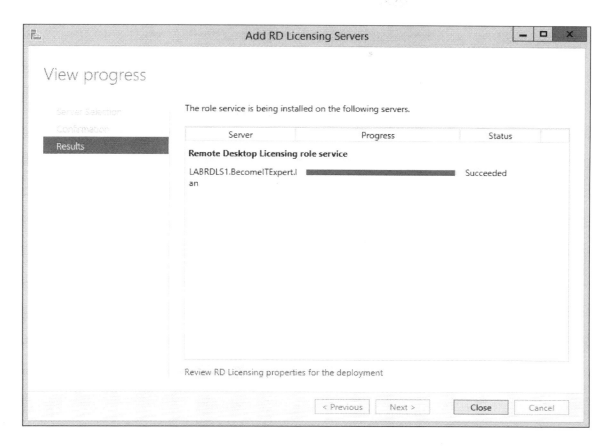

- Under "**DEPLOYMENT SERVERS**", check that the new RDLS Server "LABRDLS1" was correctly added to the RDS deployment:

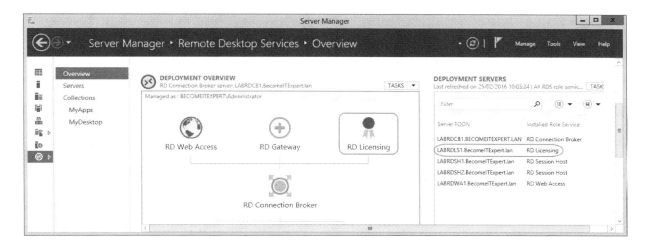

- Finally, open a Windows session on the LABRDLS1 server and check the availability of a new GUI management tool named "**Remote Desktop Licensing Manager**":

RD License Server post-installation tasks

Once deployed, RD License Server requires some post-installation tasks:

- Activate the RD License Server
- Add the RD License Server to "**Terminal Server License Servers**" group in AD DS.

Activate the RD License Server

Follow the instructions below to successfully activate "LABRDLS1" RD License Server:

- Open the "**Remote Desktop Licensing Manager**" console from LABRDLS1 server
- From the left pane, right-click on the root node (LABRDLS1) and select "**Activate Server**"

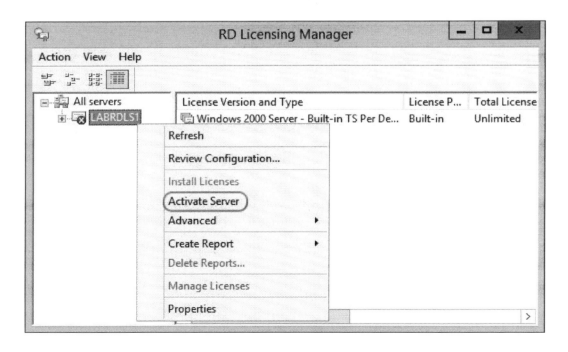

- The Activate Server Wizard is displayed, click " **Next** " to continue

- 3 Activation options are available:
    - **Automatic** : you RDLS Server is automatically activated via the Internet
    - **Telephone** : you have to call the Microsoft Activation Center to activate your RDLS Server
    - **Web Browser** : you have to activate your RDLS server via the Web Activation Platform : https://activate.microsoft.com

The "**Automatic**" activation option requires an Internet connection, so if your RD License Server is connected to Internet, simply click **Next**" automatically activate it.

If your RD License Server is not connected to Internet, you have to activate it by phone (call Microsoft Activation Center) or via the public Web Portal (Remote Desktop Licensing website).

Note that the activation via the website (Activate.Microsoft.com) can be performed from any machine connected to the Internet, including machine that are not part of your corporate network or AD domain.

To do so, go to https://activate.microsoft.com, enter the required informations (Product ID...) and finally note the generated RDLS ID then specify it on the wizard to confirm the activation of your RD License Server:

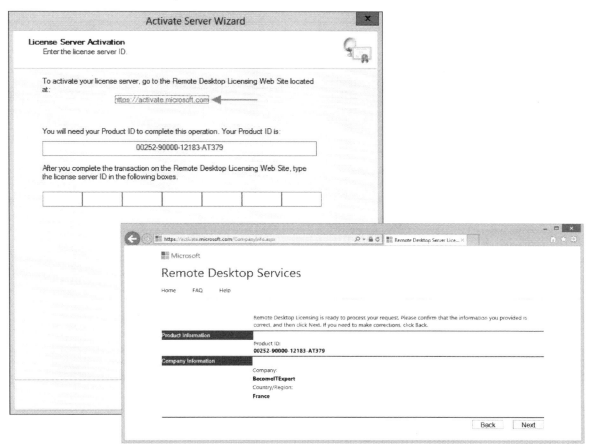

- Once the RDLS ID entered, click "**Next**" to continue:

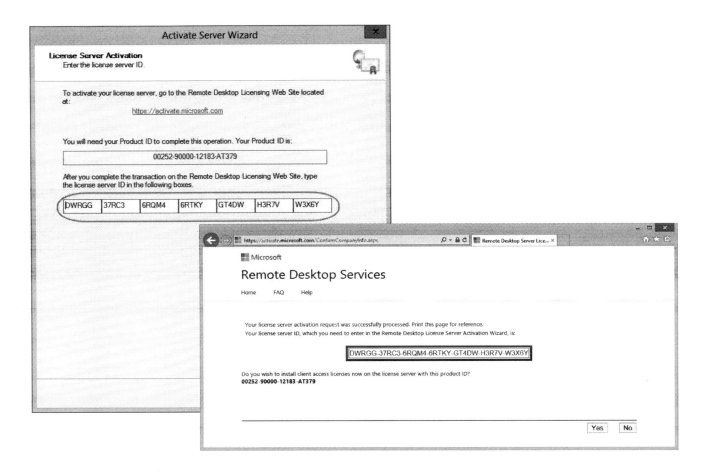

Once the RD License Server activated, the Wizard displays the following message, uncheck "**Start Install Licenses Wizard now**" and click on "**Finish**" to close the wizard:

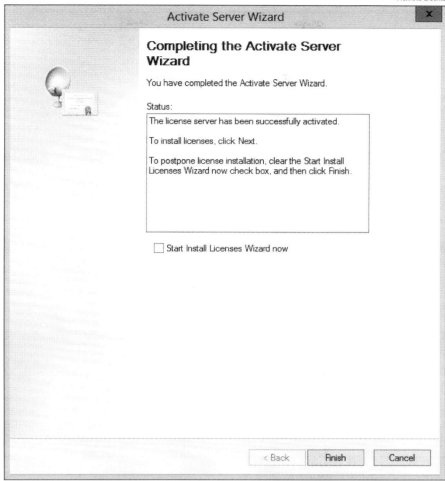

Add your RD License Server to AD Group

Follow the instructions below to successfully add your RD License Server to "**Terminal Server License Servers**" Active Directory group:

- Open the "**Remote Desktop Licensing Manager**" console from LABRDLS1 server
- From the left pane, right-click on the root node (LABRDLS1) and select "**Review Configuration...**"

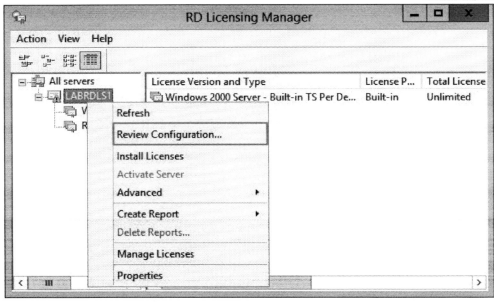

- The following dialog box will appear, then click on "**Add to Group**":

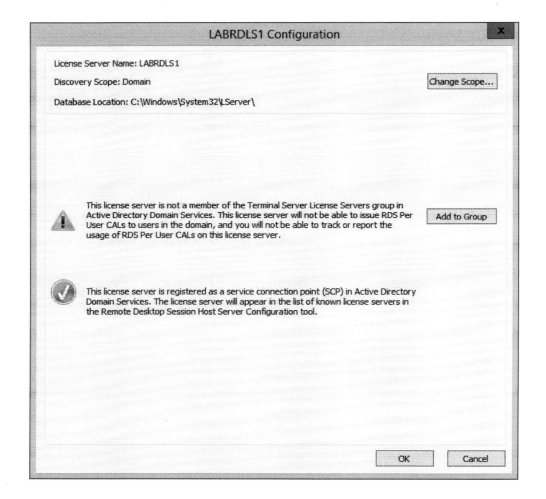

- Click on "**Continue**"
- Once added to "Terminal Server License Servers" AD group, the following message appears:

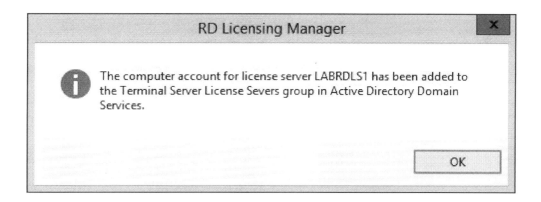

- The status of your RD License Server should look like the image below:

Install the RDS CAL

As discussed earlier, you can have up to two concurrent administrative connections to an RD Session Host server for administrative purposes. Administrative connections do not require an RDS CAL.

In Windows 8.1, like in previous Microsoft client OS versions, only one simultaneous incoming RDP connection is supported. It means that only one user (one session: remote or local) can simultaneously connect to a Windows 8.1 computer.

From the third remote desktop connection, a RD License Server as well as RDS CAL are required.

 You should have a valid RDS CALs (Per-User or Per-Device) to perform the following practical workshop.

Follow the instructions below to successfully install your RDS CAL, note that in the following example a Per-Device RDS CAL will be installed:

Install RDS CAL Automatically

- Open the "**Remote Desktop Licensing Manager**" console from LABRDLS1 server
- From the left pane, right-click on the root node (LABRDLS1) and select "**Install Licenses**"

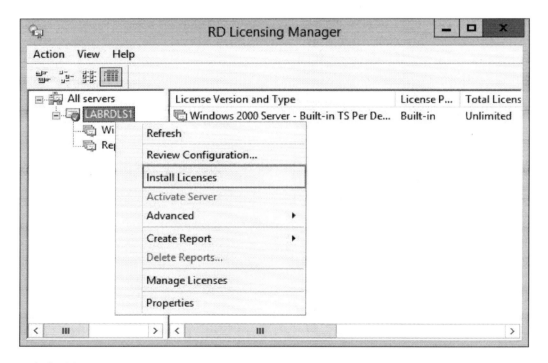

- Click "**Next**"
- On the **License Program page**, select the appropriate program through which you purchased your RDS CALs, and then click Next:

 The License Program that you selected on the previous page in the wizard determines what information you need to provide on this page. In most cases, you must provide either a license code or an agreement number. Consult the documentation provided when you purchased your RDS CALs

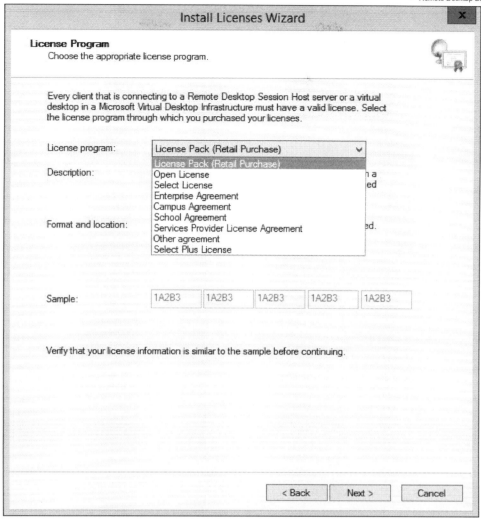

- After you have entered the required information, click "**Next**"
- On the **Product Version and License Type page**, select the appropriate product version, license type, and quantity of RDS CALs for your environment based on your RDS CAL purchase agreement, and then click "**Next**"
- The **Microsoft Clearinghouse** is automatically contacted and processes your request. The RDS CALs are then automatically installed onto the license server and the following message is displayed:

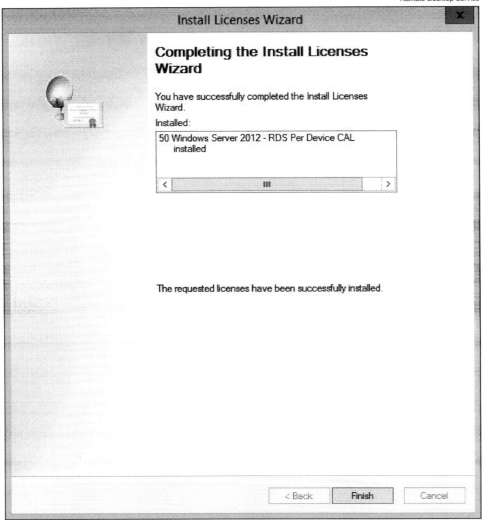

- To complete the process, click "**Finish**". The license server can now issue RDS CALs to clients that connect to a RD Session Host server

Install RDS CAL by Using a Web Browser or the Telephone

If your RD License Server is not connected to the Internet, you can install your RDS CAL using the same options detailed during the RD License Server Activation:

- ➡ Using a Web Browser
- ➡ Using the Telephone

As shown below, simply select "**Install client access licenses**" and follow the instructions of the Web Wizard:

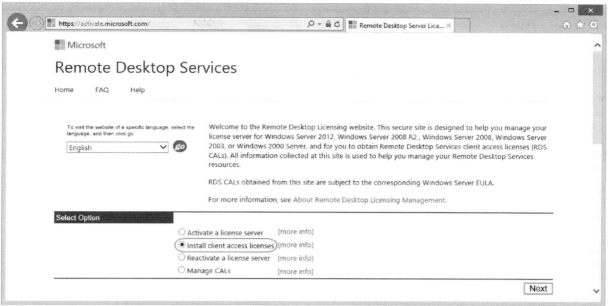

- Once installed, RDS CAL now appear as a new entry on the "**Remote Desktop License Manager**"

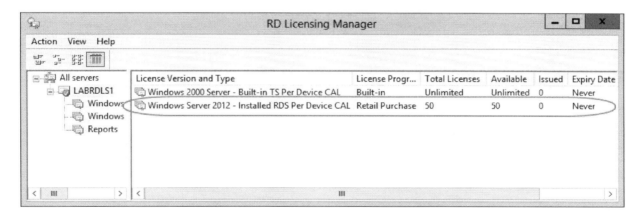

Configuring RD Session Host Servers to Use RD License Servers

After the deployment of the RD License Server and the installation of the RDS CAL, your RDS deployment is automatically configured and updated with these informations.

Indeed, the RD License Server and Remote Desktop Licensing mode is automatically specified in the RDS deployment.

Simply edit the RDS deployment, from the left pane, click on "**RD Licensing**" and check that the RDS licensing informations are correctly specified:

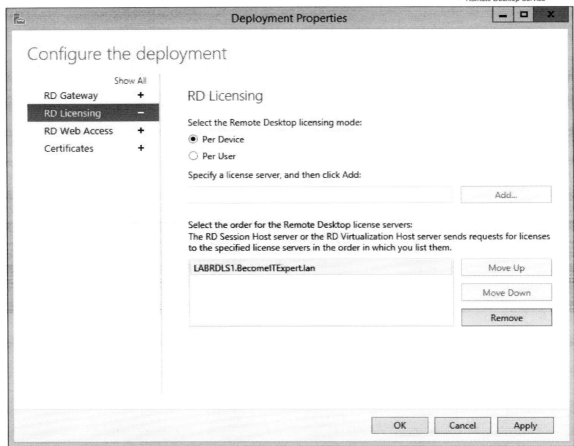

 If you have installed a Per-User RDS CAL, the "**Per User**" option is ticked.

These two options can also be configured via GPO:

Computer Configuration | Policies | Administrative Templates | Windows Components | Remote Desktop Services | Remote Desktop Session Host | Licensing

Parameters:

- Use the specified Remote Desktop license servers
- Set the Remote Desktop licensing mode

Managing and Reporting License Usage

When users log onto an RD Session Host server that is set to Per-User mode, the RD Session Host server checks to see if each user has the licensing property set in the user account properties in AD DS.

If the licensing property is set, then a user can log on; if not, the licensing server will ask the domain controller to update the user account to show that it's using an RDS CAL.

To track per-user licensing, you must have a domain. You can't find evidence of this user CAL in the user account properties in AD DS; this is not exposed in the user interface. However, you can run a report on the license server to see how many user CALs have been allocated.

To do so, open RD Licensing Manager, right-click a server, and choose "**Create Report**", Per User CAL Usage

 Only choose an activated server to create the report. The Create Report command will function even if the server has no CALs or hasn't been activated, but it will return an empty set

To generate the report, specify the part of AD DS to search for the data, as follows:

- **Entire Domain**: the domain that the license server belongs to
- **Organizational Unit**: a particular OU where user accounts are stored that is also part of the domain where the license server resides. Choose this option to restrict a search to a particular OU, if you want to get usage for only a subset of users
- **Entire Domain And All Trusted Domains**: includes domains in other forests in the search, but choosing this option will increase the time needed to generate the report

Chapter 9. Make your RDS infrastructure 2012 R2 available from the Internet

So far in this book, you have learned how to access RemoteApp programs and Remote Desktop Session Host sessions when your users are located on your internal network, but what if they want to access these resources from home, from an Internet café, or another public place?

The RD Gateway role service allows secure Remote Desktop Protocol access from clients located outside the corporate network to resources located inside the corporate network, without needing any special software on the client, as long as it supports connecting via RD Gateway

For example, RD Gateway must be deployed when you plan to allow remote access to:

- Remote Workers
- Remote Contractors
- Customers

How RD Gateway Works

RD Gateway is an RDS role service that acts as a intermediary between the external client and the internal resource that the user wants to use. It governs who is allowed to connect via RD Gateway (Connection Access Policies, or CAPs) and what resources (VM, Sessions, even physical computers) the people who are allowed to connect can use (Resource Access Policies, or RAPs).

How it Works?
1. A user wanting access to an internal RDP resource runs the RDP file pointing to that resource, whether from a saved RDP file, from RemoteApp and Desktop Connections tool, from RD Web Access, or by starting a Remote Desktop Connection (RDC) and typing in the needed information to make the connection.
2. The RDP file is configured with the RD Gateway information defined locally, or when the resource was published, and the connection request goes to RD Gateway.
3. RD Gateway first authenticates the client and verifies that the client is authorized to make this connection by checking the user credentials against its RD Connection Access Policies (RD CAPs).

4. If the client is authenticated and authorized, RD Gateway then verifies that the client is allowed to connect to the requested resource by checking its RD Resource Access Policies (RD RAPs).
5. If the client is allowed access to the requested resource, RD Gateway establishes an RDP connection to the resource. Thereafter, all traffic for this connection is passed through RD Gateway, as shown below RD Gateway forwards packets back and forth from the RD Session Host server and the remote client, sending RDP packets over port 3389 to the internal RDP resource, and Secure Sockets Layer (SSL)–encapsulated packets over port 443 to the remote client:

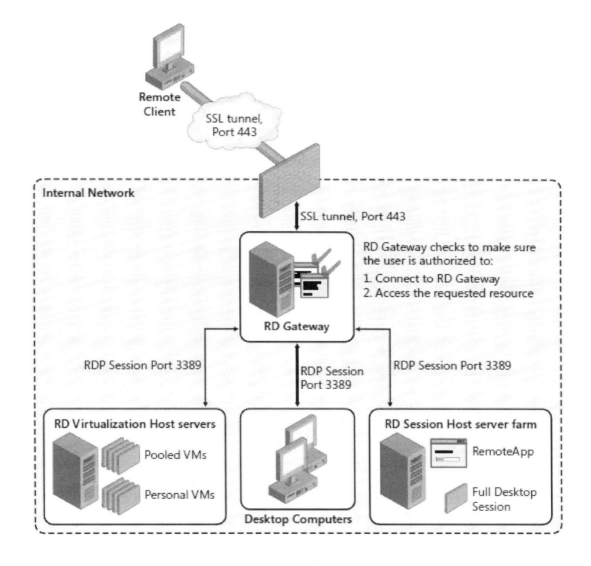

Understanding RD Gateway Authorization Policies

RD Gateway uses two distinct types of authorization policies, in consecutive order, to control connections to internal RDP resources. First, the connecting client's user, and

optionally computer credentials, are checked against RD CAPs to see that the connecting client is allowed to access RD Gateway Specifically, RD CAPs define:

- Which users (specified by user group membership) can connect to RD Gateway
- From which computers (specified by computer group membership) users can connect (optional)
- Supported authentication methods (smart card or password)
- Which client devices will be redirected to the remote session
- Optional timeouts for active and idle sessions

RD CAPs are stored in a Network Policy Server (NPS), part of the Network Policy and Access Services role in Windows Server 2012 R2. The Network Policy and Access Services role is installed automatically when you install RD Gateway; if you like, you can select to store the RD CAPs on a central NPS to allow multiple RD Gateway servers to draw their RD CAPs from the same server (This also makes sense if you're using NPS for other reasons).

After the RD Gateway has established that its RD CAPs allow the user to connect, it checks the resource requested against its RD RAPs. RD RAPs specify which internal resources (specified by computer groups) a user is allowed to access via RD Gateway. This two-tiered system makes it possible to specify, for example, that a user can connect via the Internet but cannot connect to his or her desktop computer via RD Gateway, even though he or she can do so when connecting from the local area network (LAN).

Think of RD CAPs and RD RAPs as specifying who can get to what. RD CAPs define who can connect to RD Gateway, and RD RAPs define what internal resources user groups can connect to after they connect to RD Gateway.

You can have multiple RD CAPs and RD RAPs in use at the same time. A user must meet the requirements specified on at least one RD CAP and one RD RAP to connect to RD Gateway and then to do anything after that.

To use RD Gateway, you must create at least one RD CAP and one RD RAP, but you might need more than one of each to control access to RD Gateway and to network resources more explicitly. Defining multiple RD CAPs and RD RAPs allows you to be very specific when granting network access instead of giving clients full access to every RDP-enabled device on the network that they could get to while on the LAN.

It's easiest if you group RD CAPs and RD RAPs conceptually. For instance, you can use two RD CAPs and two RD RAPs to specify the following connection requirements:

- **Company Marketing Team Remote Access Authorization Policies:**

- o RD CAP Marketing user group members can establish a connection to RD Gateway, but only when they are using computers that belong to the Marketing computer group. These users can connect only using smart cards, and device redirection will be disabled
- o RD RAP Marketing group users can then connect only to Marketing computers as well as the company RDS farm
- Company Sales Team Remote Access Authorization Policies
    - o RD CAP Sales user group members can connect to RD Gateway from any computer. They can use password authentication, and clipboard and printer redirection are allowed
    - o RD RAP Sales user group members can connect to computers that are members of the Sales computer group

RD Gateway Requirements

RD Gateway is an RDS role service and therefore runs on Windows Server 2012 R2. Hardware requirements can vary, depending on the load the role service will accommodate, but in general, RD Gateway can accommodate a large number of concurrent connections on standard server hardware.

For example, RD Gateway capacity planning information provided in the Windows Server 2012 R2 guide shows that a dual processor server with 4 GB of RAM can accommodate more than 1200 connections.

It's a so worth noting that RD Gateway can be virtualized.

To implement RD Gateway, you will need certificates that allow the client and RD Gateway to set up a trusted communications channel, and the clients will need to use a supported operating system and RDP client.

First, you will need a certificate for RD Gateway to use. For RD Gateway and remote clients to establish an encrypted connection to one another, you must install a server authentication certificate (an SSL certificate) in the RD Gateway server certificate store. You can get the certificate from a public Certificate Authority (CA), or if you maintain your own Public Key Infrastructure (PKI), you can generate your own server authentication certificate.

Installing RD Gateway

Follow the instructions below to successfully deploy the RD Gateway:

- Open a Windows session on the DC "**LABDC1** " and launch the Server Manager
- Add the server "**LABRDG1**" to the Servers Pool (All Servers pane):

- Under "**Remote Desktop Services**" and "**DEPLOYMENT OVERVIEW**", click on the "**RD Gateway**" + button:

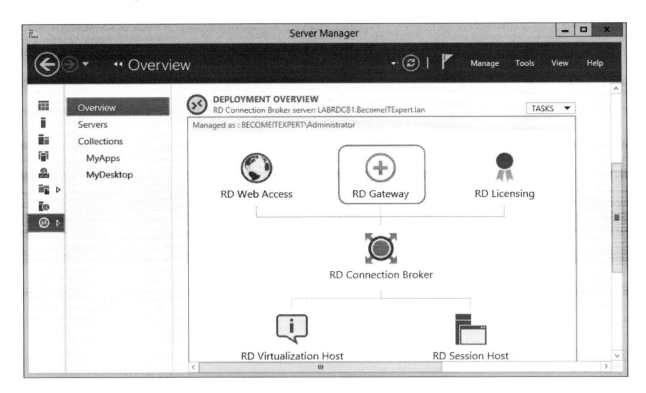

- Select and add "LABRDG1" server and then click "**Next**" to continue:

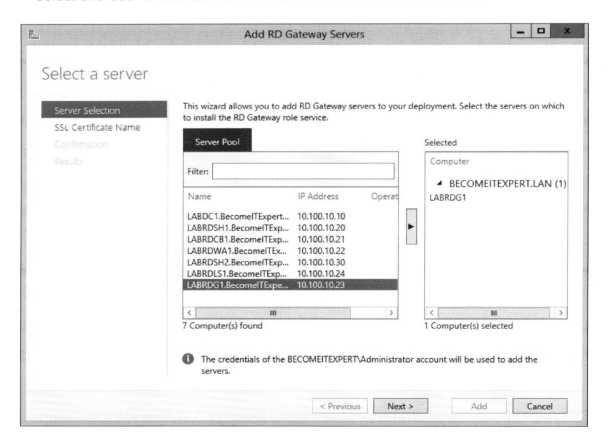

- As discussed earlier, a SSL certificate is required to implement the RD Gateway. As shown below, the "**Add RD Gateway Servers**" wizard allow you to generate and configure a new self-signed SSL certificate for your RD Gateway server. The SSL certificate name must match the FQDN of the RD Gateway Server, "**LABRDG1.BecomeITExpert.Lan**" will be used as a certificate name:
    - *Note:* in our case, the RD Gateway Server will first be used in internal (local) network. If it must allow access to external users, the external (public) FQDN must be assigned to the RDG SSL certificate

- Click "**Add**" to add LABRDG1 server to the deployment:

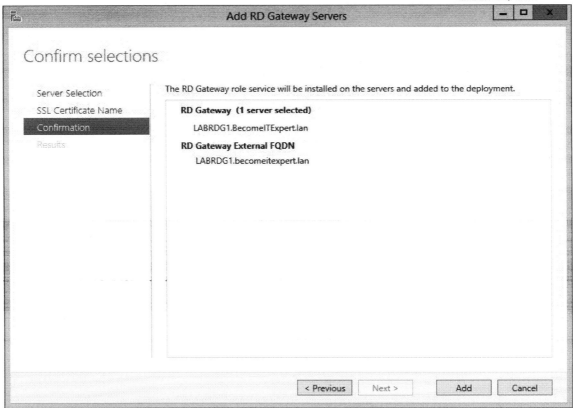

- Once added, click on "**Close**" to exit the Wizard:

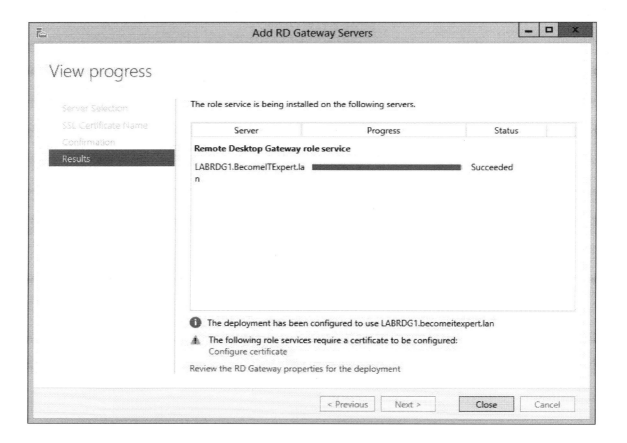

- Finally, open a Windows session on the LABRDG1 server and check the availability of a new GUI management tool named "**Remote Desktop Gateway Manager**":

Once launched, the "Remote Desktop Gateway manager" console looks like the image below:

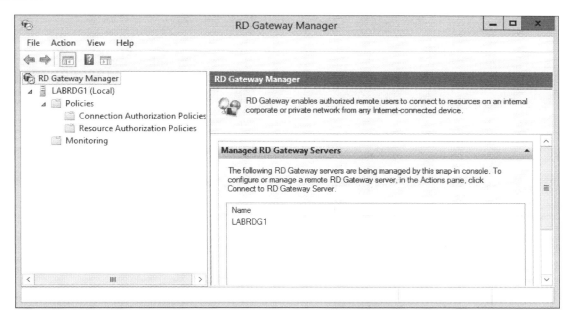

Note that this tool is included in **RSAT** (Remote Server Administration Tools) and can be installed on any network machine (Admin PC) to manage your RD Gateway Server (create and manage RD CAP & RAP Policies) remotely.

RD Gateway Server post-installation tasks

Once the RD Gateway Server deployed, two policies are created by default (one CAP & one RAP), expand and navigate to **LABRDG1>Policies>Connection Authorization Policies** and check the availability of the default policy: **RDG_CAP_AllUsers**

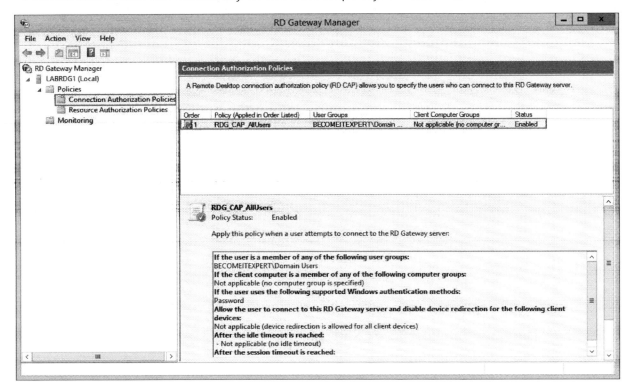

This CAP policy allows all domain users to connect via LABRDG1 RD Gateway Server.

We will edit the Policy's Properties to change its name and allow the connection via the RD Gateway only for "RDSUsers" group instead of all "Domain users". To do so:

- Right-click on the policy and select "**Properties**", under "**General**" tab, replace the default name by "**RDG_CAP_RDSUsers**":

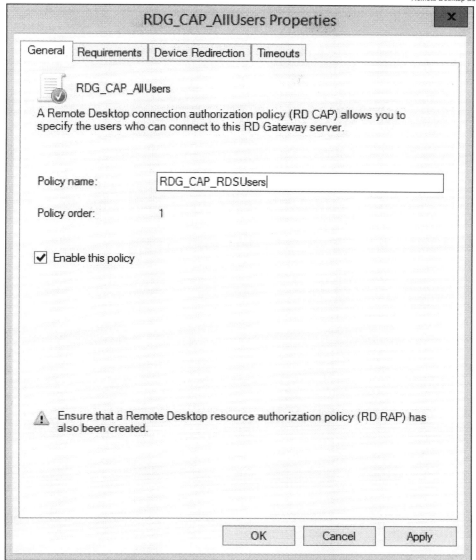

- Under "**Requirements**" tab, click on "**Add a Group...**", locate and select "**RDSUsers**" AD group:

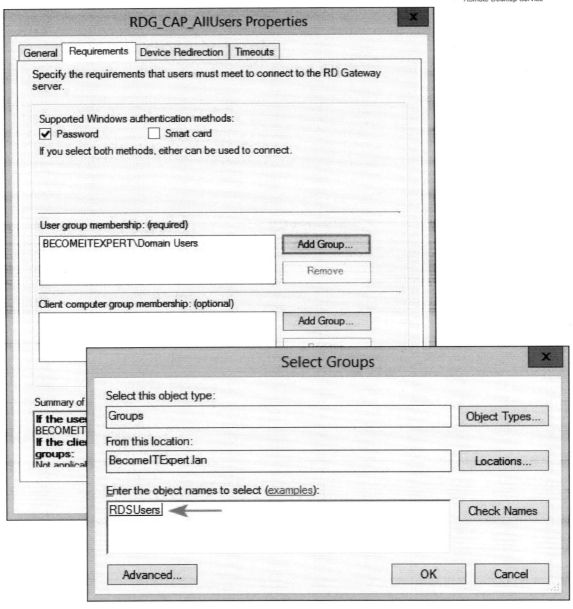

- Now select and remove the default group "**Domain Users**"
- Under "**Device redirection**", you can enable or disable Devices and Local Resources redirection, if Device redirection is enabled for all client devices, the restrictions related to Device redirection configured on the RDS Collection properties is applied:

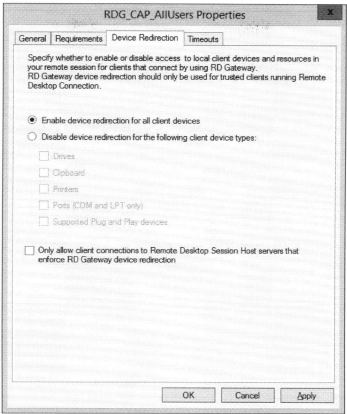

- Finally, under "**Timeouts**" tab you can specify timeout and reconnection settings for remote sessions:

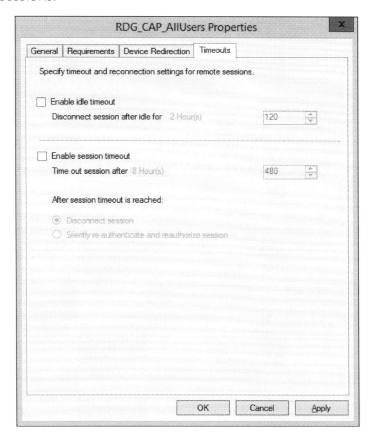

Now expand and navigate to LABRDG1>Policies>Resource Authorization Policies and check the availability of the default policy: RDG_AllDomainComputers

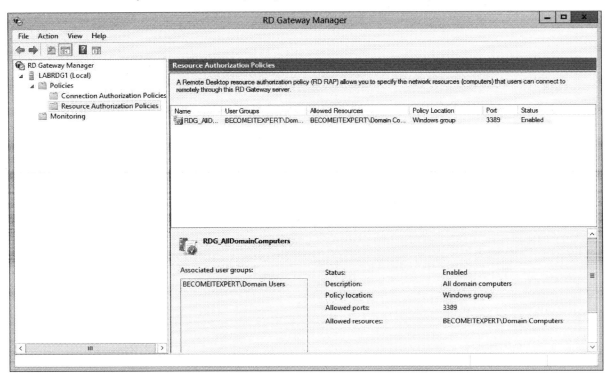

This RAP policy allows all domain users to access all internal resources (all domain computers).

We will edit the Policy's Properties to change its name and allow access to RDSH servers only (that are part of our MyApps Collection) and for "RDSUsers" group instead of all "Domain users". To do so:

- Right-click on the policy and select "**Properties**", under "**General**" tab, replace the default name by "**RDG_RAP_RDSUsers**":
- Replace the default description by : **this RAP policy allows access to RDSH Servers that are part of "MyApps" Collection for only "RDSUsers" group**

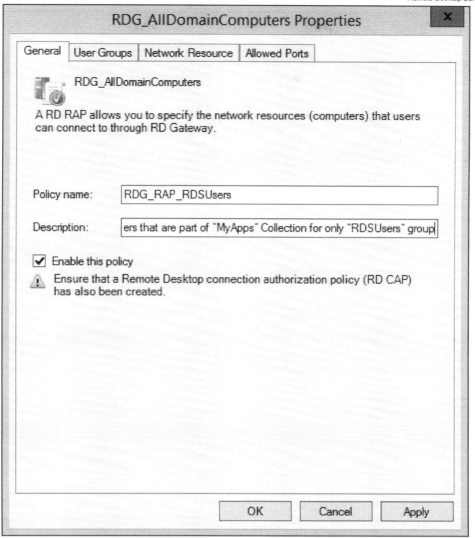

- Under "**User Groups**", click on "**Add...**", then locate and select "**RDSUsers**" AD group
- Select and remove the default group "**Domain Users**":

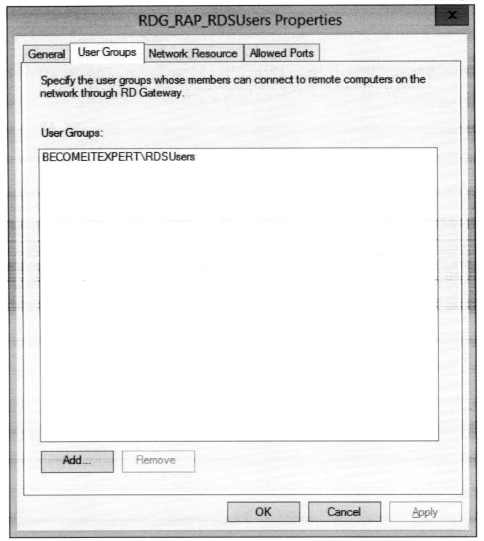

- Now, open **DSA.MSC** tool (Active Directory Users and Computers Snap-in), create a new security group named "**RDSHServers**" to which you will add the "**LABRDSH1**" server
- Under "**Network Resource**", click on "**Browse...**" and then locate and select "**RDSHServers**" security group :

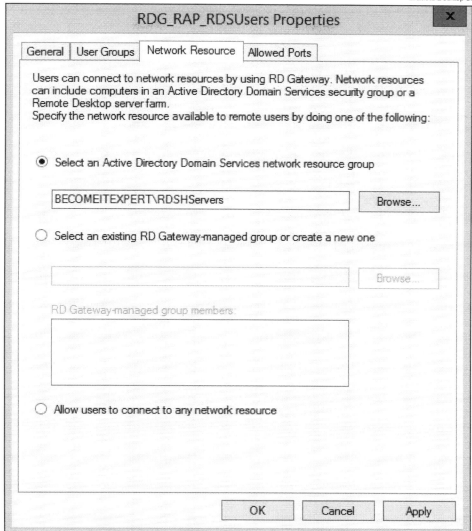

- If another port(s) than 3389 (RDP : default port) are configured in your RDS deployment, click on "**Allowed ports**" tab and check "**Allow connections to these ports**" option then enter the ports that must be used:

 If you want to specify more than one port, type the port numbers separated by a semi-colon (e.g: 3389;3390;3391)

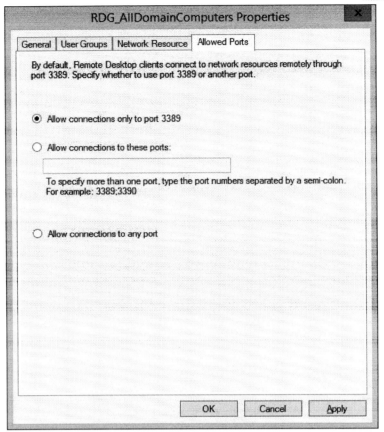

 If the RD Gateway role service is deployed using the "**Add Roles and Features**" Wizard, the default CAP & RAP policies are not created.

The RD Gateway Manager includes an advanced options that allow you to:

- Configure the number of simultaneous connections allowed
- View, Import or create a SSL certificate for the RD Gateway Server
- Configure the Network and Transport settings
- Enable logging for the RD Gateway events

All these advanced options can be configured from the RD Gateway Properties.

To do so:

- Right-click on "LABRDG1" node and select "**Properties**" or click on "**Properties**" command available from the "**Actions**" pane:

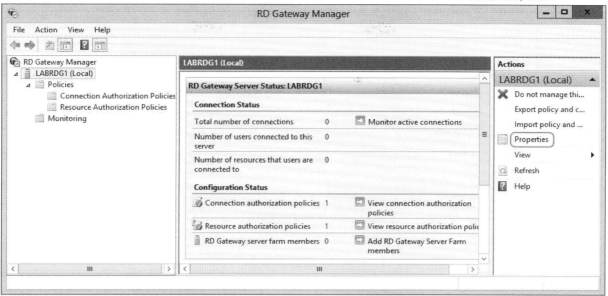

- Under the "**General**" tab, you can configure (limit) the maximum allowed simultaneous connections, the number of the allowed simultaneous connections must correspond to the number of the external users that will connect to the internal resource via the RD Gateway Server:

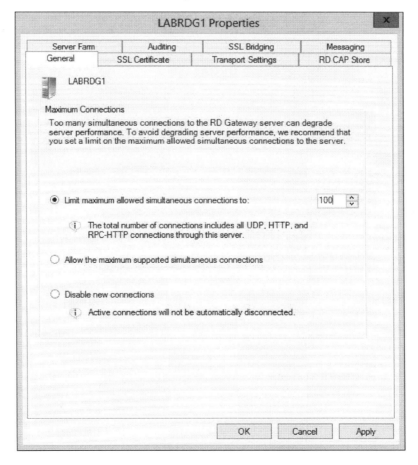

- The "**SSL Certificate**" tab includes options that allow you to view the current used SSL certificate as well as its expiration date, you can also create a new self-signed certificate or import an existing SSL certificate from the RD Gateway Certificates Store (Local Computer\Personal):

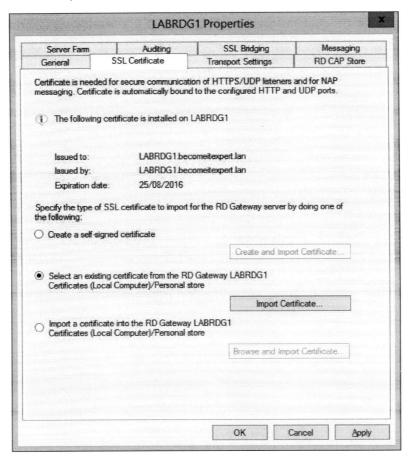

- HTTP/UDP Transport settings can be configured from the "**Transport Settings**" tab. In a production environment, the RD Gateway Server being exposed overt the Internet must have at least two Network Interface Cards (NIC): Public NIC & Private NIC.
  The HTTP transport must use the Public IP address and UDP the Private IP address:
  - *Note:* in our LAB environment, only one IP address (Private) is used

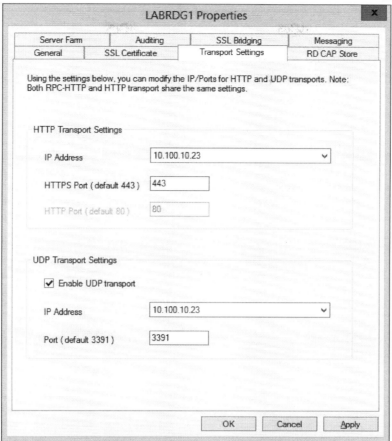

- The "**Auditing**" tab allow you select all RD Gateway events to log, such as :
    o Successful Connection Authorization
    o Successful Resource Authorization
    o Failed Connection Authorization
    o Failed Resource Authorization
    o Successful User Disconnection from the Resource
    o ...

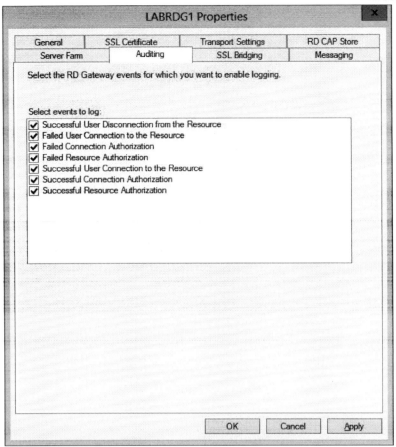

- The "**Messaging**" tab allows you to enable a "**System and Logon messages**". System and Logon messages can be added to RD Gateway in Windows Server 2012 R2 and displayed to the remote desktop user. System messages can be used to inform users of server maintenance issues such as shutdown and restarts. Logon messages can be used to display a logon notice to users before they gain access to remote resources.

 To activate a Logon message, you have to create a text file, type the message you want to display at logon for remote users and then click on "Browse..." button and finally select your text file.

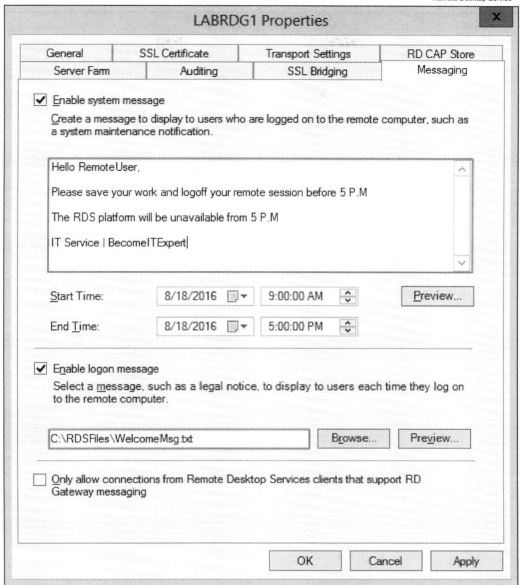

Once deployed, the RD Gateway server must be configured (specified) on your RDS deployment. In order to do so:

- Edit the RDS deployment (Under **DEPLOYMENT OVERVIEW > TASKS > EDIT DEPLOYMENT**), from the left pane, click on "**RD Gateway**"
- Tick "**Use these RD Gateway server settings:**" and enter the RD Gateway server name (**LABRDG1.BecomeITExpert.LAN** in our case):

 In order to test your RD Gateway server in local network, uncheck the "Bypass RD Gateway server for local addresses" option:

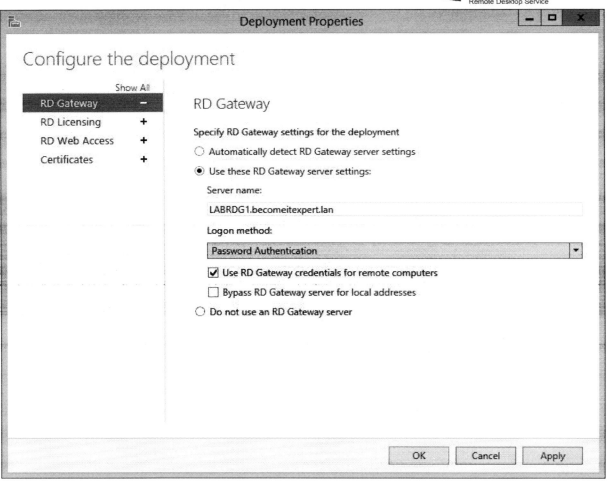

Chapter 10. Configuring Remote Desktop Services roles for High Availability

What is Load Balancing and how it works?

Load balancing refers to efficiently distributing incoming network traffic across a group of backend servers, also known as a "Server Farm" or "Server Pool".

A load balancer acts as the "traffic cop" sitting in front of your servers and routing client requests across all servers capable of fulfilling those requests in a manner that maximizes speed and capacity utilization and ensures that no one server is overworked, which could degrade performance. If a single server goes down, the load balancer redirects traffic to the remaining online servers. When a new server is added to the server group, the load balancer automatically starts to send requests to it.

In this manner, a load balancer performs the following functions:

- Distributes client requests or network load efficiently across multiple servers
- Ensures high availability and reliability by sending requests only to servers that are online
- Provides the flexibility to add or subtract servers as demand dictates

Hardware vs Software Load Balancers

Load balancers typically come in two flavors: hardware-based and software-based. Vendors of hardware-based solutions load proprietary software onto the machine they provide, which often uses specialized processors. Software solutions generally run on commodity hardware, making them less expensive and more flexible.

➪ Hardware Load Balancers

Hardware load balancers rely on firmware to supply the internal code base (the program) that operates the balancer. Hardware balancers include a management provision to update firmware as new versions, patches and bug fixes become available.

Below are some examples of Hardware load balancers:

- NetScaler | Citrix
- Alteon | Radware
- ACE | Cisco
- BIG-IP | F5 network
- ALOHA | Exceliance

⇨ Software Load Balancers

There are two types of Software Load Balancers:

Native Features in Windows Server 2012 and 2012 R2

- **NLB (Network Load Balancing)**: distributes traffic across several servers by using the TCP/IP networking protocol. By combining two or more computers that are running applications into a single virtual cluster, NLB provides reliability and performance for web servers and other mission-critical servers.

  The servers in an NLB cluster are called hosts, and each host runs a separate copy of the server applications. NLB distributes incoming client requests across the hosts in the cluster. You can configure the load that is to be handled by each host. You can also add hosts dynamically to the cluster to handle increased load. NLB can also direct all traffic to a designated single host, which is called the default host.

  NLB allows all of the computers in the cluster to be addressed by the same set of IP addresses, and it maintains a set of unique, dedicated IP addresses for each host. For load-balanced applications, when a host fails or goes offline, the load is automatically redistributed among the computers that are still operating. When it is ready, the offline computer can transparently rejoin the cluster and regain its share of the workload, which allows the other computers in the cluster to handle less traffic. Microsoft NLB uses "**NLB.sys**" Driver that's placed by default in: **C:\Windows\System32\Drivers**.

- **DNS RR (DNS Round-Robin)**: DNS Round-Robin is a local balancing mechanism used by DNS servers to share and distribute network resource loads. You can use it to rotate all resource record (RR) types contained in a query answer if multiple RRs are found.

  By default, DNS uses round robin to rotate the order of RR data returned in query answers where multiple RRs of the same type exist for a queried DNS domain name. This feature provides a simple method for load balancing client use of Web servers and other frequently queried multihomed computers.

  If round robin is disabled for a DNS server, the order of the response for these queries is based on a static ordering of RRs in the answer list as they are stored in the zone (either its zone file or Active Directory).

Free (Open Source) Load Balancing Software

Free Load Balancing Software generally work in the same way as Windows NLB feature.

Below are some examples of Free Load Balancing Software:

- HAProxy
- NGINX
- PEN
- IPVS
- ZEN Load Balancer

Configuring HA for RDSH role service

To ensure High Availability (HA) of your RDSH component and more specifically the access to your published resources (RemoteApp Program, Remote Desktop, Virtual Desktop), you have to add at least 2 RDSH servers (configured identically) by Session Collection.

According to the total number of your remote users, you might add additional RDSH servers to your Session Collection to meet your Business needs.

In our case, an additional RDSH server (LABRDSH2) will be used to ensure the High Availability of our "MyApps" Session Collection.

All RDSH servers that will be part of the same Session Collection must be configured identically: same OS version, Service Pack, Feature Pack, published RemoteApp Programs version /path...

Follow the instructions below to successfully add the second RDSH server (LABRDSH2) to the existing RDS deployment:

- Open a Windows Session on the DC "**LABDC1**" and launch the Server Manager
- Add the "**LABRDSH2**" server to the Servers Pool (All Servers pane)
- Click on "**Remote Desktop Services**" and then select "**Collections**"
- Under "**HOST SERVERS**" and "**TASKS**", select "**Add RD Session Host servers**":

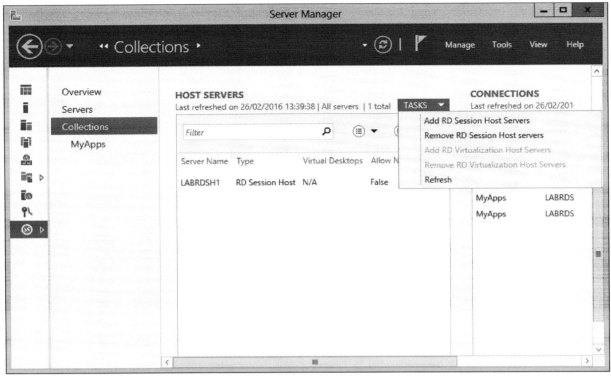

- Select and add "**LABRDSH2**" server and then click "**Next**" to continue :
    o *Note:* If LABRDSH2 server is already part of an existing Collection (e.g MyDesktop), you must delete it from that collection to be able to add it to a new one (MyApps).
- Check that the server "**LABRDSH2**" has been added and then click "**Close**".
- Now click on "**MyApps**" Collection, under "**HOST SERVERS**", click on "**TASKS**" and select "**Add RD Session Host Servers**":

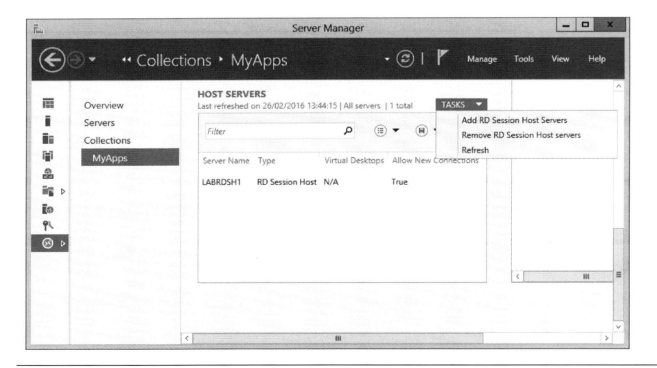

- The following Wizard appears, select and add the "**LABRDSH2**" server and then click "**Next**":

- Click "**Add**" to add LABRDSH2 server to "**MyApps**" Collection :

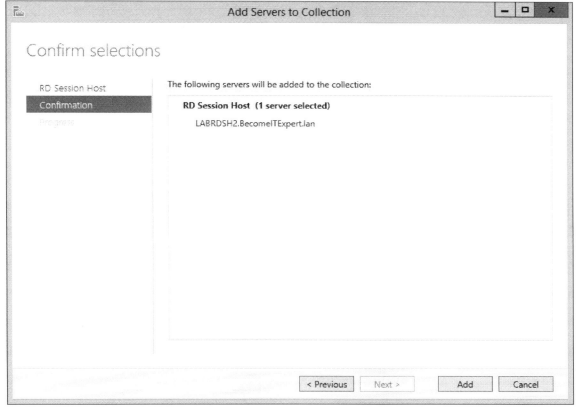

- Check that the LABRDSH2 server is added successfully and click "**Close**" to exit the Wizard:

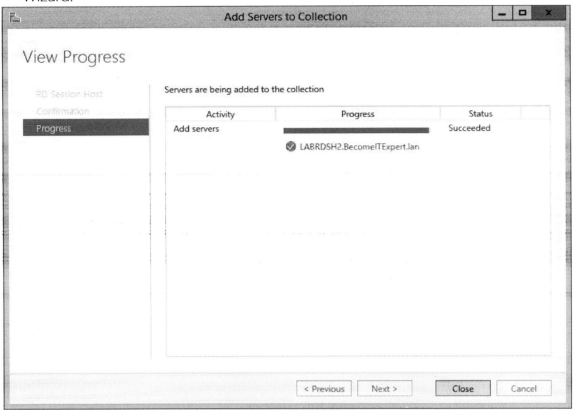

- The "**MyApps**" Session Collection now contains two RD Session Host : **LABRDSH1** and **LABRDSH2**:

- Load balancing options can be configured from the Session Collection properties: select "**MyApps**" Collection, under "**PROPERTIES**", click on "TASKS" and select "**Edit Properites**"

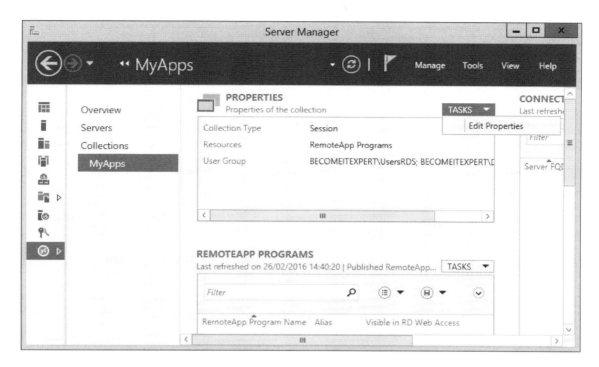

- In the following example, the options below will be configured
    - Relative Weight   : 50/50
    - Session Limit   : 60 Session per RD Session Host server
- Once the "**MyApps Properties**" Wizard is displayed, click on "**Load Balancing**" pane and configure both "**Relative Weight & Session Limit**" options as detailed above : spread the load between the RDSH servers to 50/50 mode and limit the number of remote desktop sessions to 60 by RDSH server:

 If needed, edit the Collection Properties and increase the maximum number of session per RDSH server.

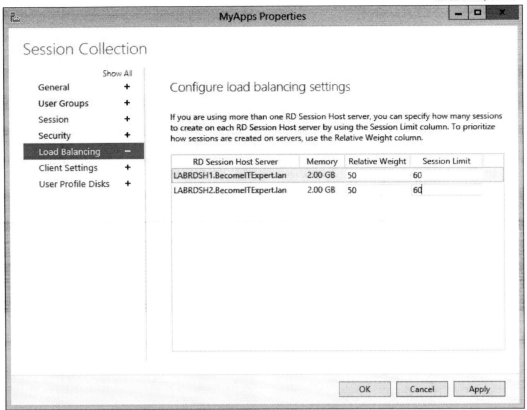

- Finally, to test your RDSH high availability, power off the first RDSH Server "LABRDSH1 server" or simply disconnect it from the network (disable its vNIC) to make it unreachable and test the redundancy of the RDSH role service.

Configuring HA for RDWA role service

In some scenarios, RD Web Access is presented as being a critical service that must be available 24/7/365.

Indeed, some organizations offer access to different users (internal & external), partners, and customers to their internal resources only via the RDWA Portal.

To ensure High Availability for RDWA role service, Windows NLB Feature will be used.

Note: *for more informations about using Hardware load balancers with RDWA, refer to technical documentations available on the Hardware LB manufacturer.*

Follow the instructions below to correctly configure HA for the RDWA role service:

Note: *a new server named "LABRDWA2" has been deployed and joined to our AD domain*

- Open a Windows Session on the DC "**LABDC1**" and launch the Server Manager
- Add the server "**LABRDWA2**" to the Servers Pool (All Servers pane):

- Click on "**Remote Desktop Services**", under "**DEPLOYMENT OVERVIEW**", right-click on "RD Web Access" and select "**Add RD Web Access Servers**":

- Select and add "**LABRDWA2**" server and then click "**Next**" to continue
- Verify that the server "**LABRDWA2**" has been added and then click "**Close**".

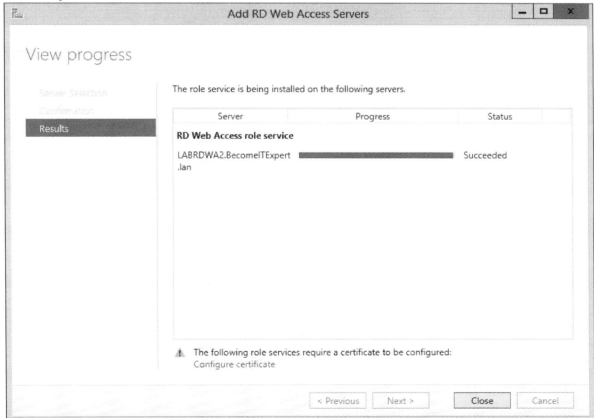

- Now that the second RDWA server is added to our RDS deployment, we will install Windows NLB feature on both RDWA servers, to do so : open Windows PowerShell from LABDC1 (as Administrator) and enter the following command to remotely install the NLB feature on "LABRDWA1 & LABRDWA2" servers as well as the NLB Manager console:

Invoke-Command -ComputerName LABRDWA1,LABRDWA2 -ScriptBlock{Install-WindowsFeature NLB -IncludeManagementTools}

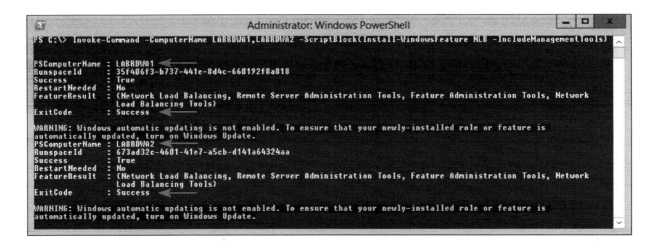

- Once NLB feature is installed on both RDWA servers, we will now create a new NLB Cluster that will include LABRDWA1 & 2 servers. In order to do so :
- Open a Windows Session on the "**LABRDWA1**" server and open the NLB manager by entering **NLBMgr.exe** from "*Run*" Menu:

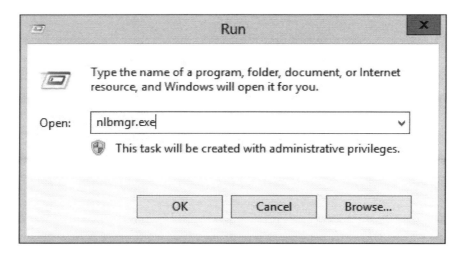

- Right-click on the root node and select "**New Cluster**":

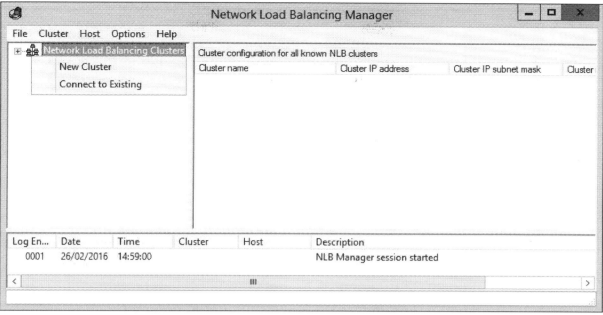

- Specify the NetBIOS name of the first Cluster Node (LABRDWA1 Server) and click on "**Connect**", the LABRDWA1 Interface name and its associated IP address are listed, click on "**Next**" to continue:

 In a production environment, Microsoft recommends two NICs per node: e.g ADMIN & PROD NICs.

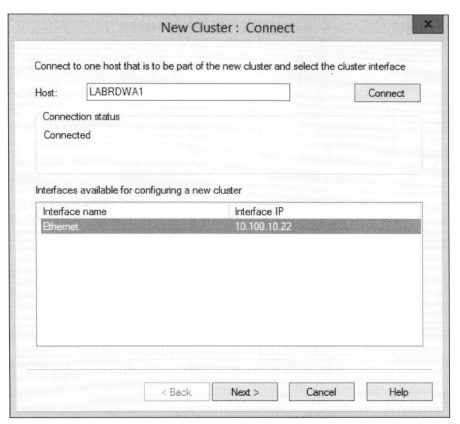

- Leave the default settings and click "**Next**":

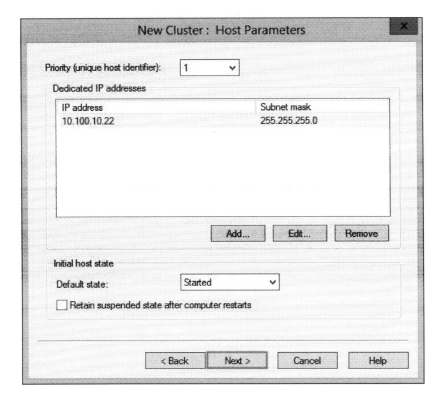

- Click on "**Add...**" button and specify an IP address for the NLB Cluster (check the availability of the IP address before assigning it to NLB Cluster), then specify the subnet mask and click "**OK**":
    - o Note : in the following example, **10.100.10.100/24** will be assigned to the NLB Cluster

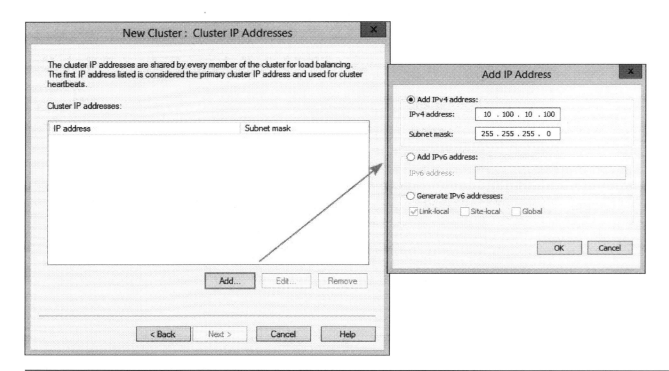

- Click "**Next**" to continue:

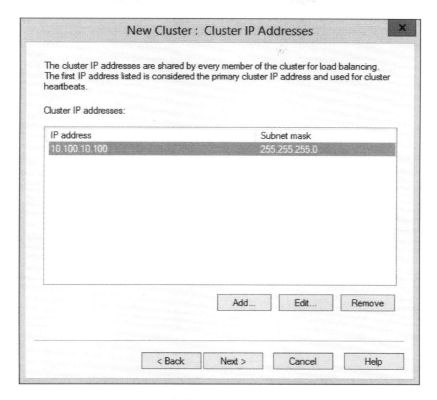

- Specify a NLB Cluster FQDN and click "**Next**" to continue, in the following example "**PortalApps.BecomeITexpert.lan**" is used as a NLB Cluster Full internet Name

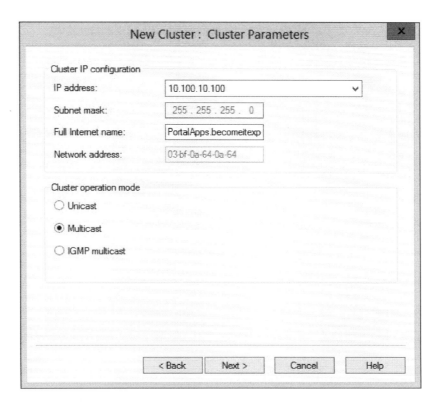

 If your RDWA Portal must be accessible from the Internet, you have to use a "Public" full Internet Name, such as **"PortalApps or AppsPortal.MyCompany.com"**. In this case, your RDWA Portal name must be reachable from the Internet.

- Leave the default settings and click on "**Finish**":

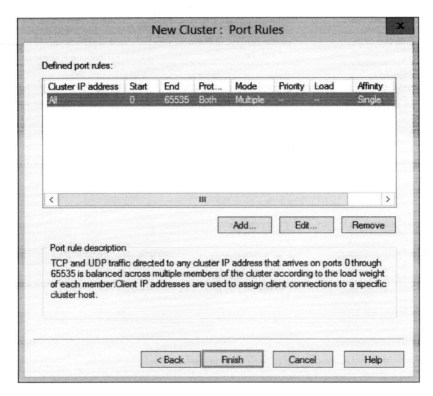

- You can configure the NLB Cluster mode (**Active/Active** or **Active/Passive**) by clicking on the "**Edit**" button. In our case, the "**Active/Passive**" mode will be used, so the "**Single Host**" option is ticked:

 For more informations about Windows Server 2012 R2 Network Load Balancing (NLB) feature, refer to the following link: https://technet.microsoft.com/en-us/library/hh831698(v=ws.11).aspx

- The NLB Cluster "**PortalApps.BecomeITExpert.lan**" is created and contains a single node (**LABRDWA1** server):

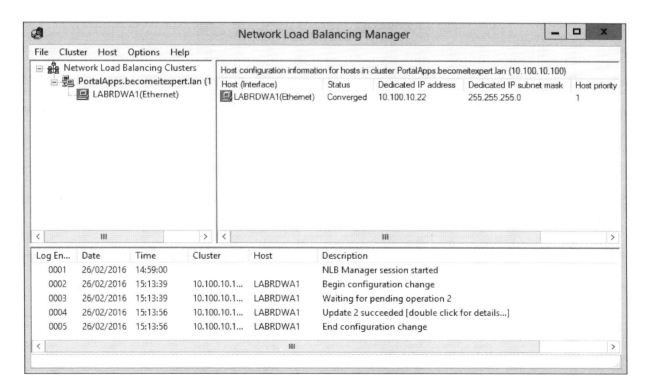

- Now, we will add the second node (**LABRDWA2** server) to the NLB cluster created previously. To do so, open a Windows Session on the "**LABRDWA2**" server and launch the NLB Manager "**NLBMgr.exe**":

- Right-click on the root node and select "**Connect to Existing**":

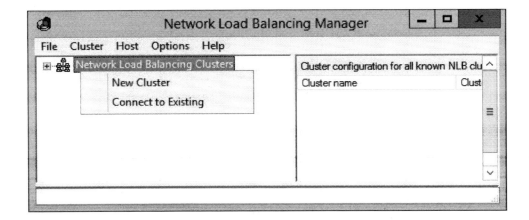

- Enter the NetBIOS name of the first node "LABRDWA1" and click on "**Connect**", check that the existing NLB Cluster name "PortalApps.BecomeITExpert.lan" is displayed. Then click "**Finish**" to exit the Wizard:

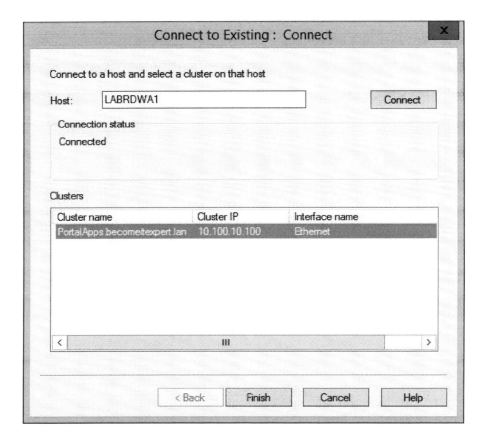

- Now right-click on the "**PortalApps.BecomeITExpert.lan**" node and select "**Add Host to Cluster**":

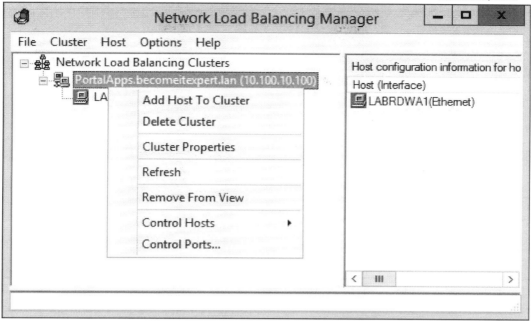

- Enter the NetBIOS name of the second node (LABRDWA2) and click on "**Connect**", and then click "**Next**" to continue:

- Check that the second host priority is set to "2" and its default state is "**Started**" and click "**Next**" to continue:

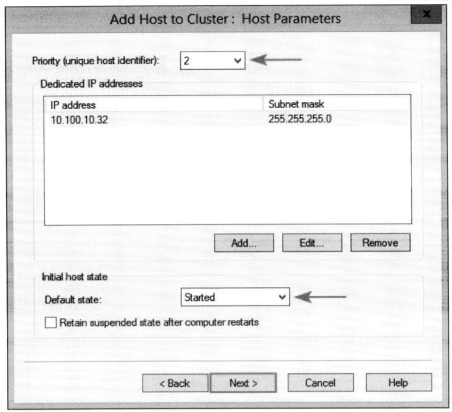

- Leave the default settings and click on "**Finish**":

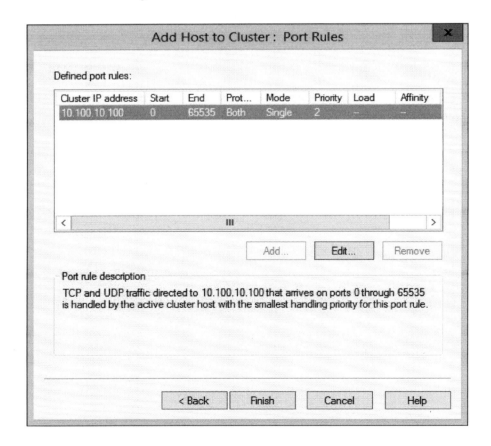

- Our NLB cluster "**PortalApps.BecomeITExpert.lan**" now contains two nodes (two hosts) : LABRDWA1 & LABRDWA2:

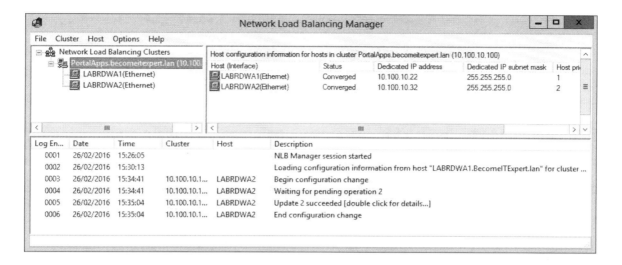

- Finally, a new DNS host corresponding to the NLB Cluster name must be created "manually". In order to do so, open a **DNS Manager** console from the DC "**LABDC1**", expand "**Forward Lookup Zones**", right-click on "**BecomeITExpert.lan**" zone and then select "**New Host (A or AAAA)...**", the following dialog box appears, create a new Host with the following informations :
    o   Name   : PortalApps
    o   IP address   : 10.100.10.100

Note: there is a known Network issues with Windows NLB Feature when used on VMware Workstation environment. Our RDS lab infrastructure is hosted on <u>Hyper-V 2012 R2</u> server.

- Now open a Windows Session on "**LABW81**" client and connect to https://PortalApps.BecomeITExpert.lan/RDWeb using Internet Explorer

- The DNS name "PortalApps" corresponds to NLB Cluster IP address, so the web traffic is redirected to one of the NLB Cluster node (LABRDWA1 or LABRDWA2):

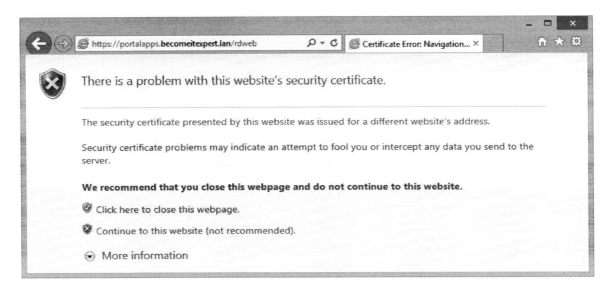

- Click on "**Continue to this website (not recommended)**" to continue
- As shown below, the Web traffic is redirected to "LABRDWA1" server because the NLB Cluster is in Active/Passive mode (the first node "LABRDWA1" is still Up):

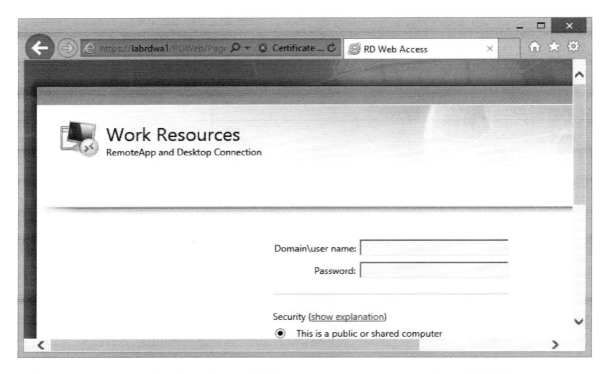

- To test the high availability of your RDWA role service, power off the LABRDWA1 server or simply disable its virtual NIC and then try to reconnect to RDWA Portal using https://PortalAppsBecomeITExpert.LAN/RDWeb URL

- Open the NLB Manager console and check that the status of the first node (LABRDWA1) is "Unreachable", the second node (LABRDWA2) takes over and becomes the active host in the NLB Cluster:

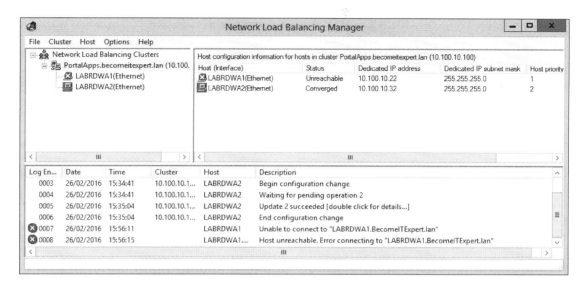

- When you connect to https://PortalApps.BecomeITExpert.lan/RDWeb, Web traffic is now redirected to the second host (LABRDWA2), this allows you to ensure the service continuity and avoid any downtime:

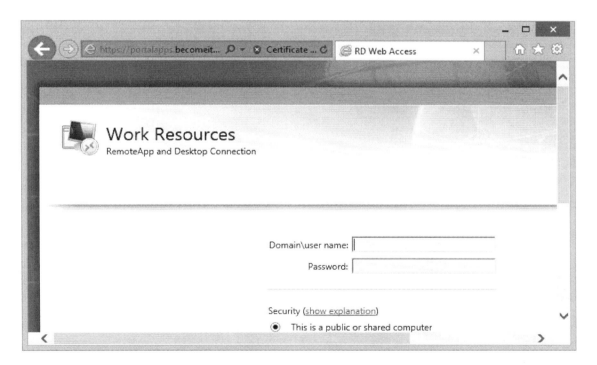

Configuring HA for RDCB role service

Contrary to RDSH and RDWA role services, there are several requirements that must be met to make your RDCB service highly available:

- You need to deploy SQL Server (2008 R2 SP1 or higher) Standard, Enterprise or Express Edition to host the RDS database in which RDCB HA configuration informations will be stored
    - *Note:* *In our case, SQL server Express Edition (free Edition) will be used.*
- You need to install SQL Server Management Studio Express to manage RDS database
- A SQL native client must be installed on each RDCB server
- You have to configure a static IP address on each RDCB server
- You have to create a DNS RR (Round-Robin) record
- You have to create a DNS Round Robin entry with all RDCB IP addresses

To ensure High Availability for RDCB role service, at least two RDCB servers must be deployed.

In our case, two new Windows Server 2012 R2 will be deployed and joined to Active Directory domain:

- **LABRDCB2**: the second RDCB server that will be add to our RDS deployment for RDCB HA
- **LABSQL1**: the SQL server (2012) that will host the RDCB HA configuration informations.

Follow the instructions below to successfully deploy the SQL server 2012 Express Edition Server and make your RDCB role service highly available.

⇨ **Deploy your SQL Server 2012 Express Edition on LABSQL1 server**

- First, download SQL Server 2012 Express and run the EXE File (as Administrator): ENU\x64\SQLEXPR_x64_ENU.exe
- Choose "**New SQL server stand-alone installation or Add features to an existing installation**"
- Check "**I accept the license terms**" and then click "**Next**" to continue
- Uncheck "**Include SQL Server product updates**" and click " **Next** " to continue
- Simply tick "**Database Engine Services**" and leave the default paths, and then click "**Next**" to continue
- Specify an instance name and leave the default instance root directory and then click "**Next**" (FARMRDS will be used as an instance name)
- Set the Startup type of the "**SQL Server Browser**" to "**Automatic**" and click "**Next**"

- Choose the "**Mixed Mode** " as an authentication method and set a new password for the SQL Server System Administrator "sa" account, then click " **Next** " to continue
- Click "**Next**" to start the installation
- Once installed, click "**Close**" to exit the installation Wizard.
- Now you have to perform some SQL Server post-installation tasks. To do this, launch the "**SQL Server Configuration Manager**" available from the Welcome Screen
- Expand "**SQL Server Network Configuration**" node and select "**Protocols for FARMRDS**". From the right pane, right-click on TCP/IP and select "**Enable**"

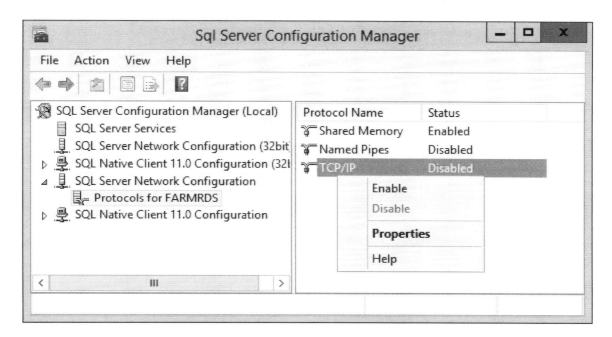

- Now right-click on TCP/IP and select this time "**Properties**", under "IP Addresses" tab, check that the TCP Dynamic Ports (under "IPAll" section) is set to **1433** and if necessary change /enter it manually.

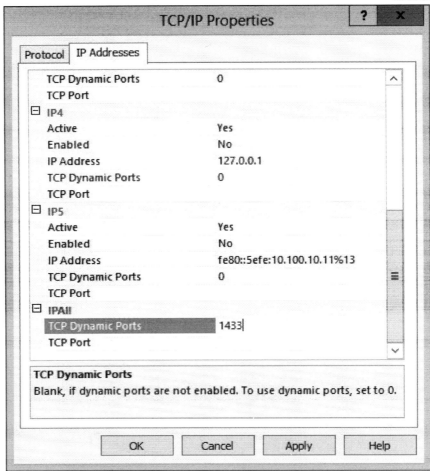

- You have now to select "**SQL Server Services**" and restart the Windows service related to the "FARMRDS" SQL instance, refer to the image below:

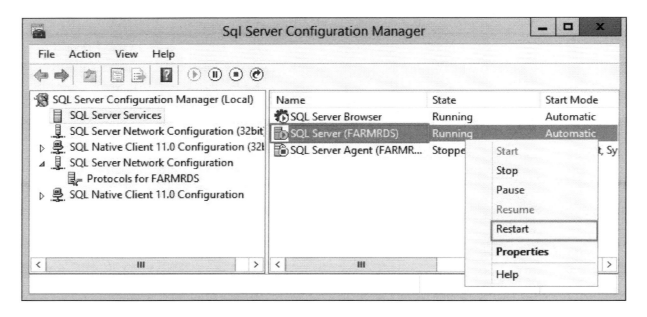

Note that all RDCB servers must be able to communicate with the SQL server (LABSQL1 server) on 1433 port, so this flow must be opened on LABSQL1 (create a new Windows Firewall Rule to allow incoming traffic to 1433 port).

⇨ Install SQL server 2012 Native Client on each RDCB server

Follow the instructions below to successfully install the SQL Server 2012 Native Client on each RDCB server (LABRDCB1 & LABRDCB2):

- Download the SQL Server 2012 Native Client > File **ENG\x64\sqlncli.msi**
- Run the downloaded MSI file and follow the installation Wizard
- Once installed, click "**Finish**" to close the Wizard.

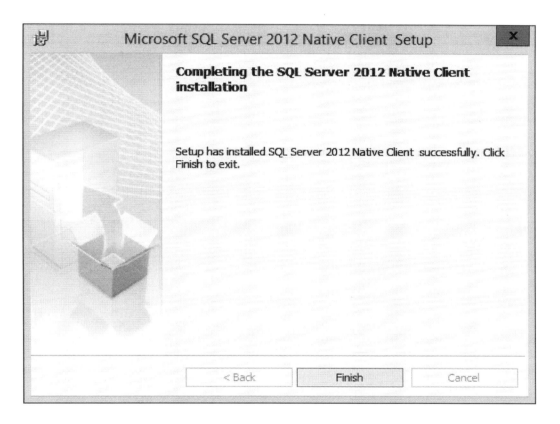

⇨ Install SQL Server Management Studio Express 2012 (SSMSE) on LABSQL1

Follow the instructions below to successfully install the SSMSE console on the LABSQL1 server:

- Download SSMSE 2012 > File **ENU\x64\SQLManagementStudio_x64_ENU.exe**
- Run the downloaded EXE file as Administrator
- Click "**New SQL server stand-alone installation or Add features to an existing installation**"
- Choose "**Add features to an existing instance of SQL Server 2012**" option, check that the FARMRDS instance is selected from the list and click "**Next**" to continue

- Tick "**Management Tools - Basic**" and click "**Next**" to continue
- The wizard will check some prerequisites and then start the SSMSE installation...
- Once installed, click "**Close**" to exit the Wizard.

When configuring RDCB role service in HA mode, a new SQL Database will automatically be created and hosted on the SQL server we just deployed (LABSQL1).

All RDCB servers that will be part of the RDCB HA configuration need a "**DBCreator**" permission on the SQL Server to be able to create and store informations on the RDS SQL Database.

Follow the instructions below to assign the "**DBCreator**" permission for both RDCB servers of our RDS deployment:

- First, create a new AD security group (RDCBServers) and add both LABRDCB1 and LABRDCB2 servers to it.
- Open the **Microsoft SQL Server Management Studio Express** console and connect to **LABSQL1\FARMRDS** SQL instance
- Expand "**Security**" node and right-click on "**Logins** ", then select "**New Login...**":

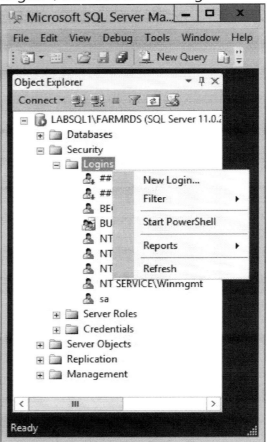

- Under "**General**", click on "**Search...**" and then locate and select the "RDCBServers" group we created previously:

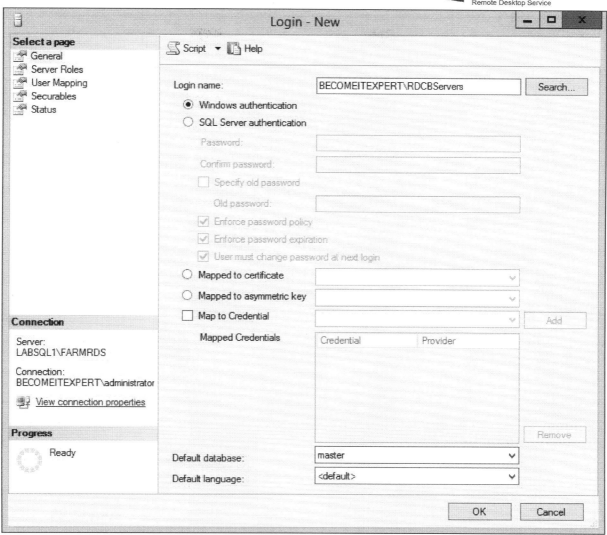

- Under "**Server Roles**", tick "**dbcreator**" and then click "**OK**":

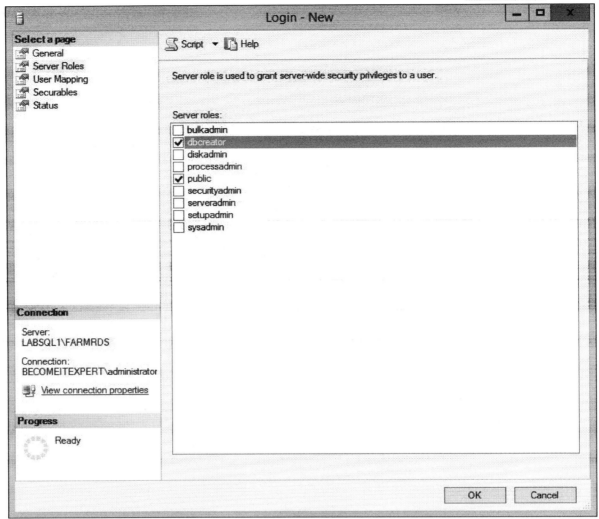

⇨ Create a DNS Round Robin entry for all RDCB IP addresses

Follow the instructions below to successfully create the DNS RR (Round Robin) entry for both LABRDCB1 /LABRDCB2 IP addresses:

- Open the "**DNS Manager** " console from LABDC1
- Expand "**Forward Lookup Zones**", right-click on "**BecomeITExpert.lan**" zone and then select "**New Host (A or AAAA)...**"
- In the following example, "**RDCBFarm**" will be assigned to the DNS RR host entry, so create two new Host (A or AAAA) named RDCBFarm and associate them to the RDCB servers IP addresses :

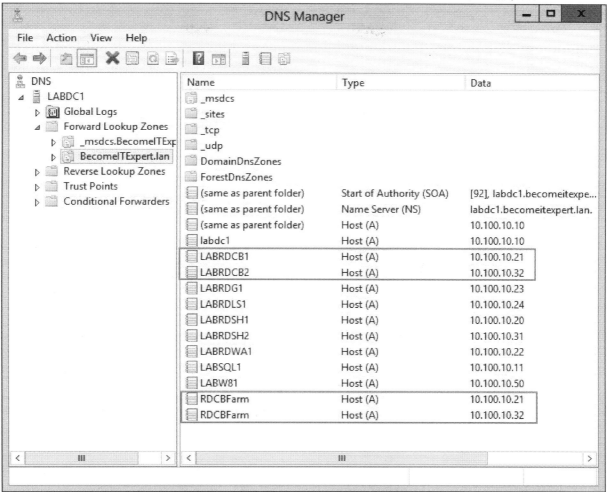

Now that all the RDCB HA requirements are met, follow the instructions below to configure High Availability for RDCB role service:

- Open a Windows session on the SQL Server "**LABSQL1**" and launch the Server Manager
- Add all RDS servers (LABRD***) to the Servers pool (from "**All Servers**" pane)
- Once added, click "**Remote Desktop Services**"
- Under "**DEPLOYMENT OVERVIEW**", make a right-click on "**RD Connection Broker**" and select "**Configure High Availability**" :

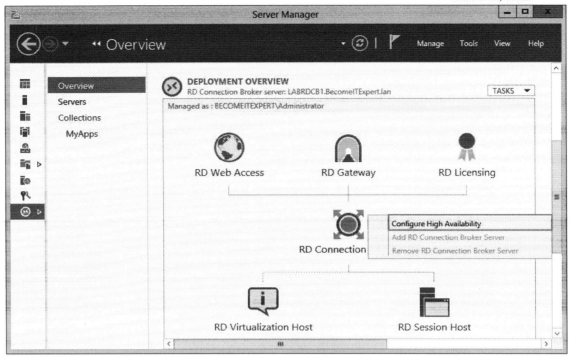

- The "**Configure RDCB for HA**" Wizard is displayed, click "**Next**" to continue
- Fill in the following informations and click "**Next**":
    - Database connection string:
        - **DRIVER**=SQL Server Native Client 11.0;**SERVER**=LABSQL1;**Trusted_Connection**=yes;**App**=Remote Desktop Services Connection Broker;**DATABASE**=RDCBDatabase
    - Folder to store the database files:
        - C:\SQLDATA
        - *Note: "C:\SQLDATA" folder should be created beforehand*
    - DNS round robin name:
        - RDCBFarm.BecomeITExpert.LAN

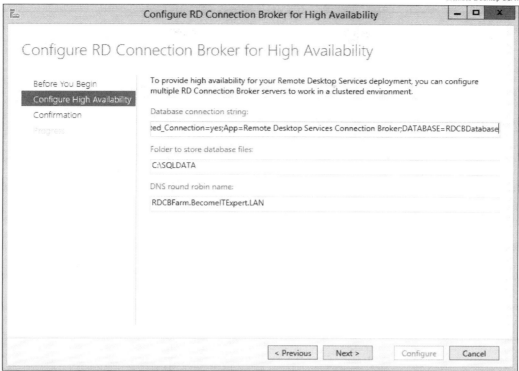

- Check the informations and click "**Configure**" to start RDCB HA configuration:

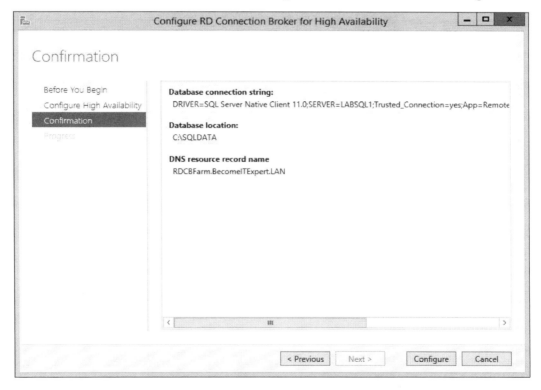

- Once RDCB HA mode is configured, the following status is displayed, click "**Close**" to exit the Wizard:

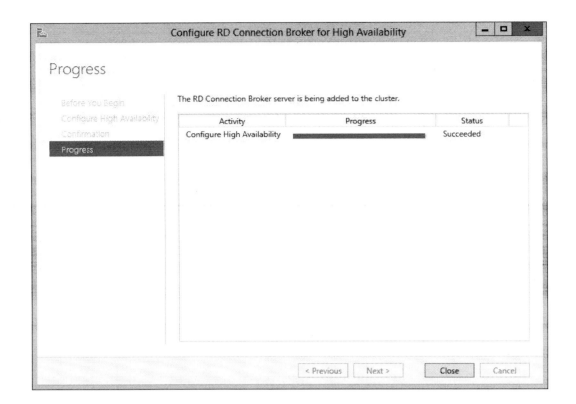

 The following error message may occur if the Database location (the folder you specified) is not accessible or restricted (if you used an UNC path).

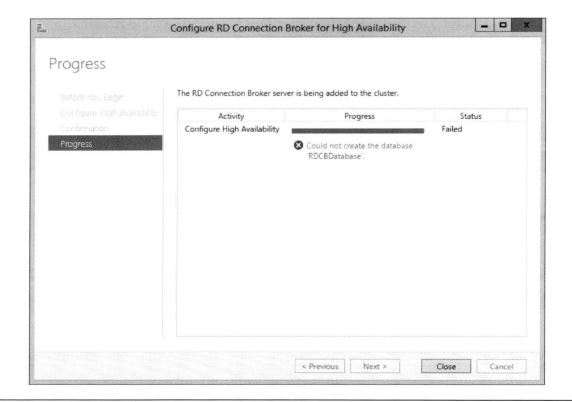

- As shown below, the RDCB role service is now configured in HA mode:

Before adding additional RDCB server(s) to your RDS deployment, you have to configure the RDCBServers AD group as a "Database Owner" of the RDCBDatabase created automatically by the RDCB HA configuration Wizard. To do so:

- Open "**Microsoft SQL Server Management Studio**" console, connect to **LABSQL1\FARMRDS** instance and then navigate to **Security > Logins**
- Locate and double-click on **"BECOMEITEXPERT\RDCBServers"** we added previously
- Under "**User Mapping**", tick **"RDCBDatabase"** and then **"db_owner"**

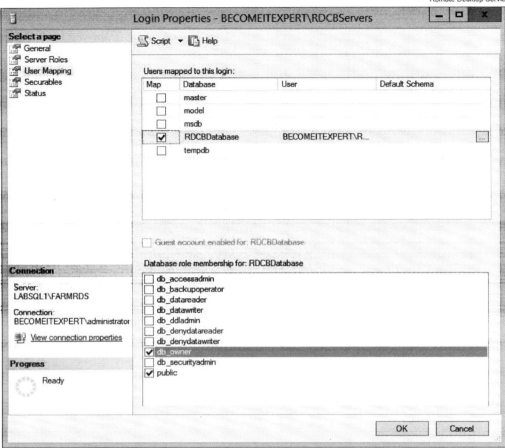

- Now we will add a second RDCB server (**LABRDCB2**) to our RDS deployment to ensure RDCB service continuity. Right-click on "**RD Connection Broker**" and select "**Add RD Connection Broker Server**":

- Select and add "LABRDCB2 " server and then click "**Add**":

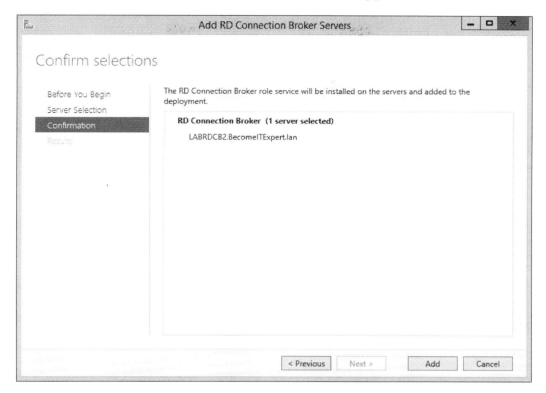

- Finally, click "**Close**" to exit the Wizard.

Now when you run a RemoteApp Program or Windows Desktop, you are redirected to the RDCB Farm (**RDCBFarm.BecomeITExpert.lan**) instead of a single RDCB server (LABRDCB1):

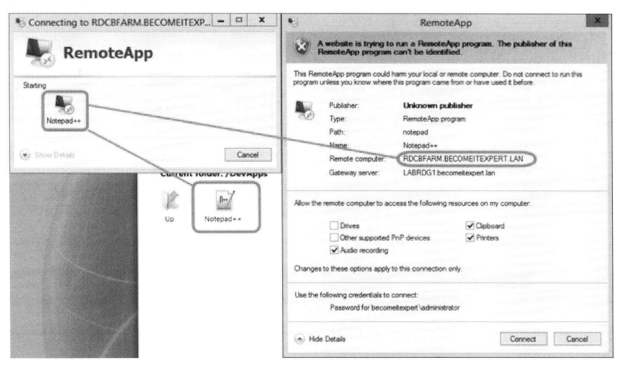

Note that only one RDCB server can be "Active" in your RDS deployment. By default, the first deployed RDCB server is configured as an "Active" RDCB server (LABRDCB1 in our case). The second RDCB server takes over and becomes Active when the first RDCB is down but you can make another RDCB server "Active" by clicking on "**TASKS**" under "**DEPLOYMENT OVERVIEW**" and clicking on "**Set active RD Connection Broker server**" option:

As shown below, the current active RD Connection Broker server is **LABRDCB1**. You can select another RDCB server from the list and click on "**Set Active**" to make it the "Active RDCB server" of the deployment:

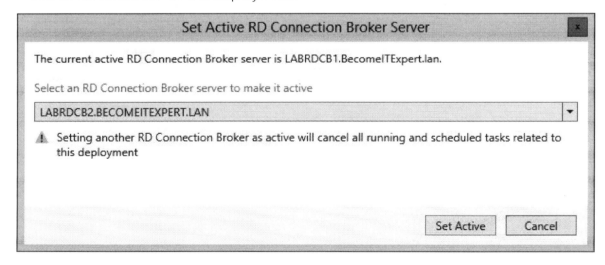

Configuring HA for RDLS role service

RD Licensing role service is best made highly available by setting up 2 or more RD licensing servers, configuring each RDSH server to use all of these RD licensing servers. The CAL's purchased should be 'split' across these RD Licensing servers. With that configuration, even if a single RD License Server is down, the RDSH server will continue to query other RD License servers to obtain a valid CAL for end users or devices.

Note that all your RDLS servers must be installed and configured identically, with the same:

- OS version /SP
- Type and number of the Installed RDS CAL type

In our case, a second RDLS server named "LABRDLS2" will be deployed and joined to our Active Directory domain.

Now we will add it to our RDS deployment, in order to do so:

- From LABDC1, open the Server Manager

- Under "**Remote Desktop Services**" and "**DEPLOYMENT OVERVIEW**", right-click on "**RD Licensing**" and select "**Add RD Licensing servers**"

- Select and add the **LABRDLS2** server and then click "**Add**". Once added, click "**Close**" to exit the Wizard:

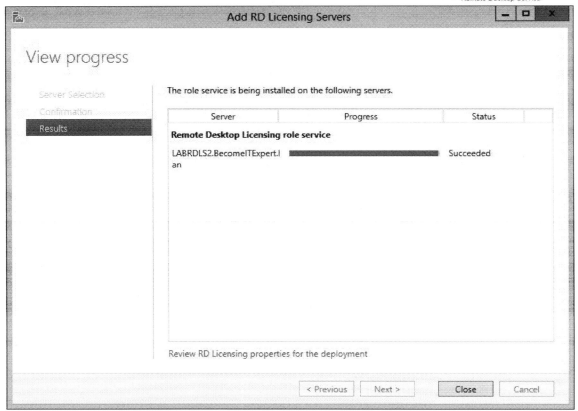

- Now that the LABRDLS2 server is added to our RDS deployment, you have to perform the same post-installation tasks described in Chapter 8. Licensing Remote Desktop Services > RD License Server post-installation tasks

Finally, check that both LABRDLS1 and LABRDLS2 servers are correctly configured in the RDS deployment properties:

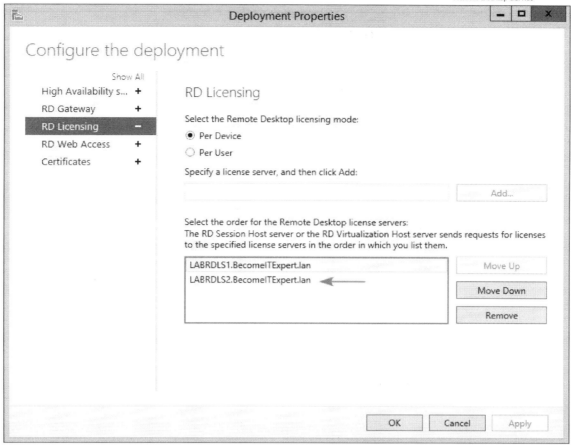

Configuring HA for RDG role service

As explained earlier, there are several Load balancing solutions (Hardware & Software) that can be used to make your RDS infrastructure highly available.

In a production environment, it's highly recommended that you use a Hardware-based solution (e.g F5 Network BIG-IP hardware solution) for your Remote Desktop Gateway.

In our case, Windows NLB will be used to make our RD Gateway highly available. In order to do, follow the instructions below:

Note: *A second RDG server (LABRDG2) has been deployed and joined to our AD domain*

- From LABDC1, open the Server Manager

- Under "**Remote Desktop Services**" and "**DEPLOYMENT OVERVIEW**", right-click on "**RD Gateway**" and select "**Add RD Gateway servers**"

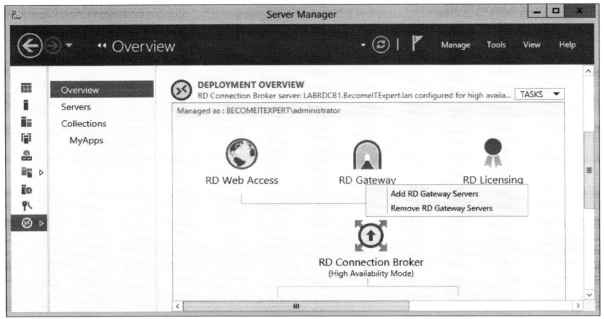

- Select and add the **LABRDG2** server and then click "**Next**".

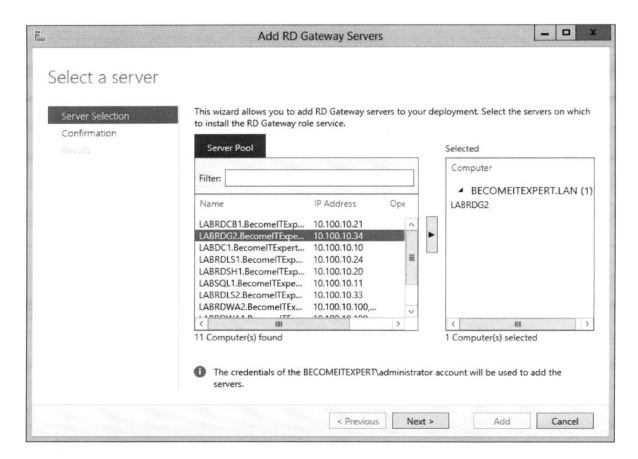

- Once added, click "**Close**" to exit the Wizard:

- Now that the second RDG server is added to our RDS deployment, we will install Windows NLB feature on both RDG servers, to do so : open Windows PowerShell from LABDC1 (as Administrator) and enter the following command to remotely install the NLB feature on "LABRDG1 & LABRDG2" servers as well as the NLB Manager console:

  Invoke-Command -ComputerName LABRDG1,LABRDG2 -ScriptBlock{Install-WindowsFeature NLB -IncludeManagementTools}

Follow the same instructions described on the "Configuring HA for RDLS role service" section to create a new NLB Cluster with the informations below:

- Cluster name   : RDGateway.BecomeITExpert.lan
- Cluster IP Address : 10.100.10.101

  o *Note:* In our example, the RDS Gateway will be used to authenticate and authorize internal users, for external users, a public internet name must be used, e.g RDGateway.mycompany.com

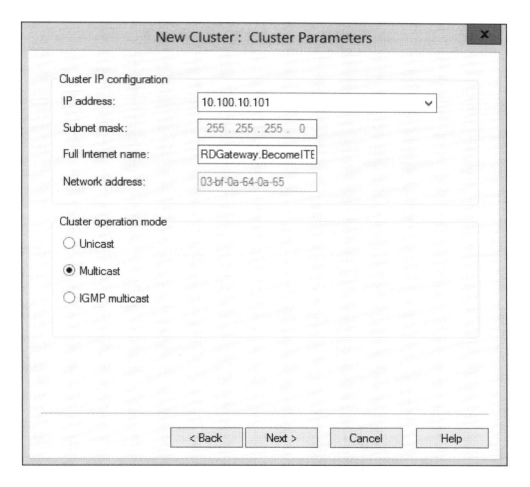

The final RDG cluster configuration should look like the image below:

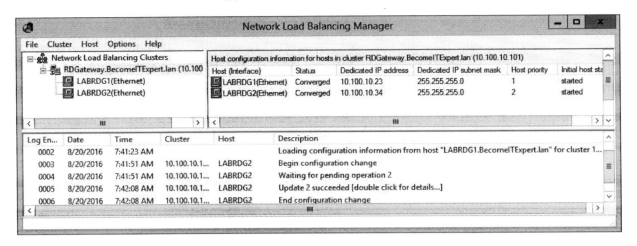

- Now you have to create (manually) a new DNS host for the NLB Cluster name. In order to do so, open a **DNS Manager** console from the DC, expand "**Forward Lookup Zones**", right-click on "**BecomeITExpert.lan**" zone and then select "**New Host (A or AAAA)...**", create a new Host with the following informations :
    o Name   : RDGateway
    o IP address : 10.100.10.101

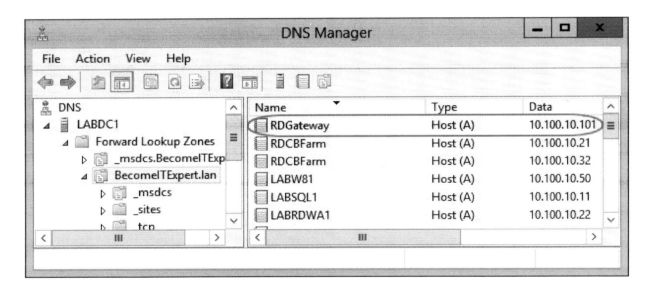

- To finish configuring HA for our RDG infrastructure, we have to add each RDG server to "Server Farm" option available on each RDG properties dialog box. Open a Windows Session on each RDG server and then launch "RD Gateway Manager" console. Right-click on the root node and select "**Properties**"

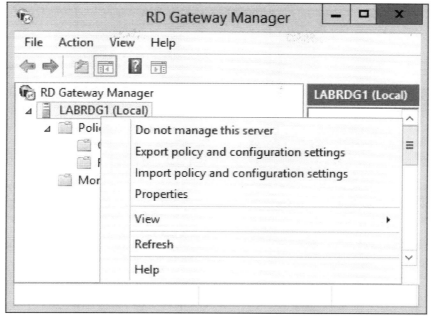

- Under "**Server Farm**" tab, add both LABRDG1 and LABRDG2 and check that their status is **OK** (click on **Refresh Status** button if needed)

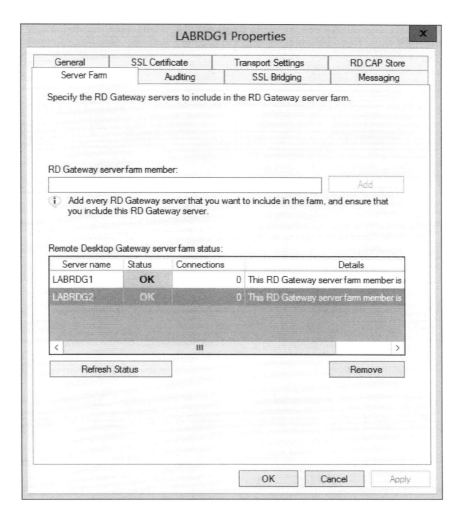

Finally, edit your RDS deployment properties and, under "RD Gateway", replace a single RDG FQDN (LABRDG1.BecomeITExpert.lan) by the RDG Farm full name (RDGateway.BecomeITExpert.lan):

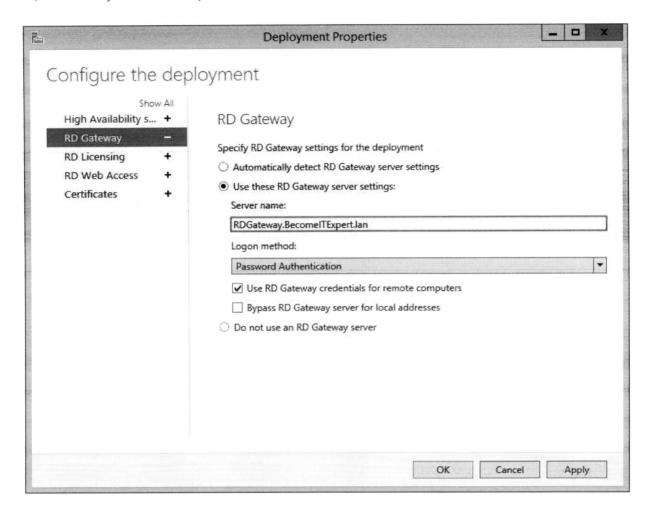

Note that you have to generate new SSL certificate that match the new RDG farm name (FQDN) and import it into your RDG certificate store.

Chapter 11. Deploying SSL Certificates

Before delivering your RDS infrastructure and make it available for your end users, You'll need to deploy SSL certificates to the roles that you're using to allow your end users to connect to RemoteApp programs or Desktops: RD Connection Broker for sure, RD Web Access, and RD Gateway if you're using it to enable connections via the Internet.

There are two types of SSL certificates you can use:

- **Self-Signed certificates** generated by the RD server itself
- **Certificates that are signed by a CA** (Certificate Authority) such as Verisign (Public CA) or an internal CA if you have your own PKI.

In our case, Self-Signed certificates will be used to secure communication between network machines and all RDS roles services.

You can deploy certificates to your RDS servers using PowerShell or RDMS. To deploy certificates via RDMS, open the **RDS Deployment Properties** and select **Certificates**.
We will first create a new SSL certificate for RDCB – SSO service, to do so, select "**RD Connection Broker – Enable Single Sign On**" and click on "**Create new certificate...**":

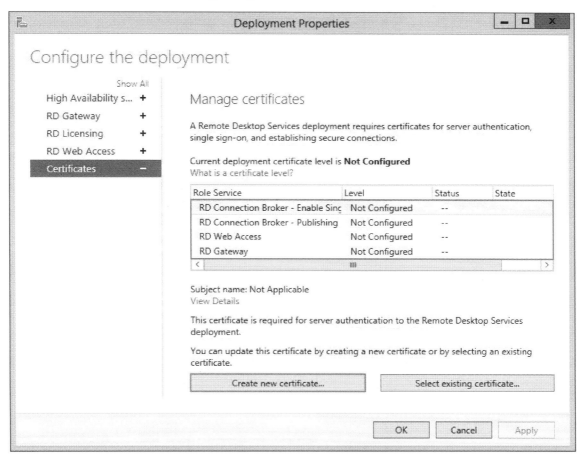

RDCB role service is configured in HA mode, so the certificate name you will specify must be the same as RDCB farm name: **RDCBFarm.BecomeITExpert.lan**

Enter a Password for the certificate, tick "**Store this certificate**" option and then enter a valid certificate path (C:\CertFiles\ in our case) where you will store the certificate pfx file. Finally, click **OK** to confirm

Note: tick "**Allow the certificate to be added to the Trusted Root Certification Authorities certificate store on the destination computers**" option:

- As shown below, once created, the certificate state becomes "**Ready to apply**". So click on "**Apply**" to validate the certificate.

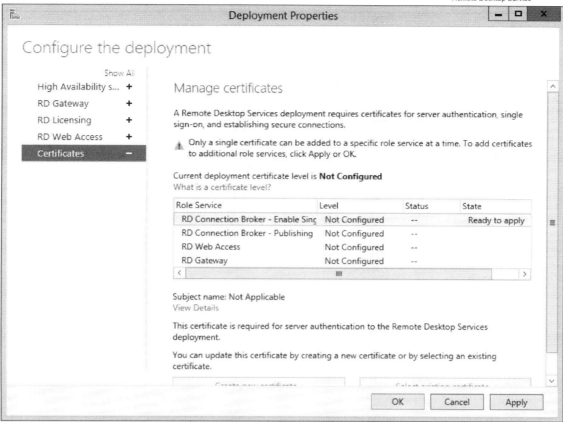

- Once validated, the certificate state becomes "**Success**"

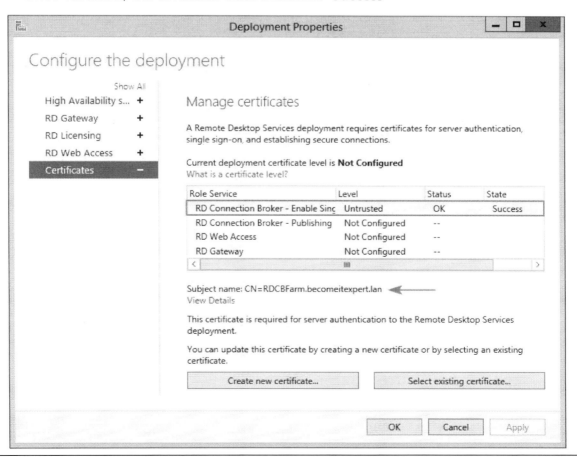

- For the **RD Connection Broker – Publishing** role service, we will import the certificate we created and exported previously. So this time, click on "**Select Existing Certificate...**" and when the dialog box below appears, select "**Choose a different certificate**" then click "**Browse...**" and select the **RDCBFarm.pfx** file

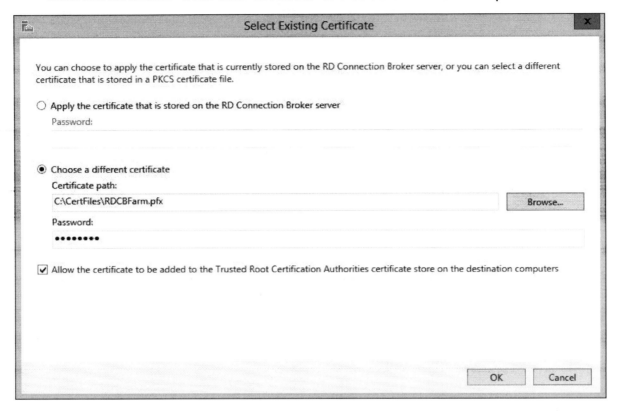

- Click OK to close the dialog box and then "**Apply**" to validate the certificate import

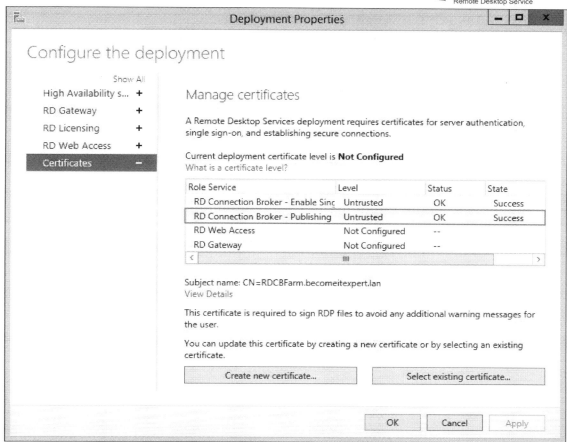

- Open a Windows session on each RDCB server and check that the certificate we created previously is present on the certificate store, in the personal store. To do so, run MMC and add "Certificates" snap-in, then connect to Local Computer (for the computer account) and finally navigate to Personal > Certificates

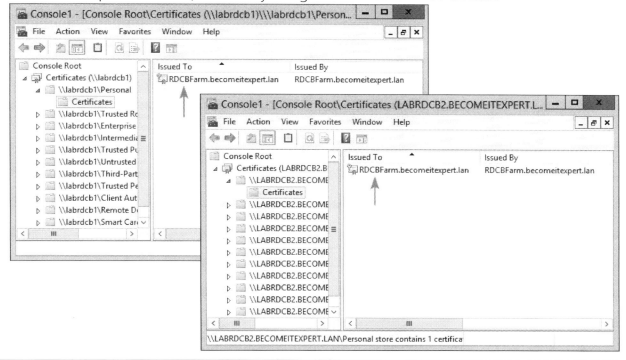

Now, repeat the same operations to create a new Self-signed SSL certificate for both RD Web Access and Gateway role services. The certificates names you will specify must match the following names:
- RD Web Access certificate name : **PortalApps.BecomeITExpert.lan**
- RD Gateway certificate name : **RDGateway.BecomeITExpert.lan**

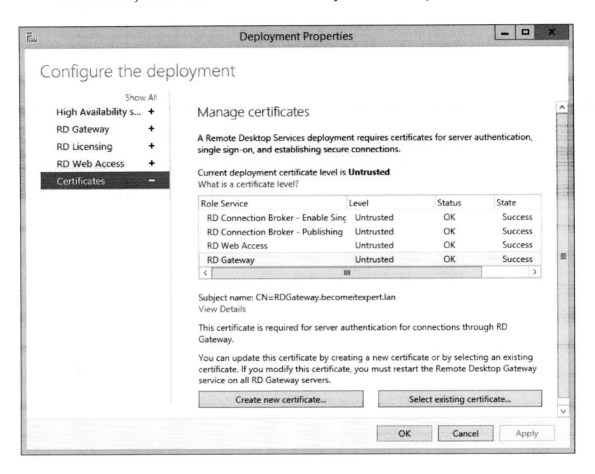

Configuring SSL certificate for RD Web Access

After deploying SSL certificate for RD Web Access servers, there is a post-deployment task that must be performed on each IIS server running on RDWA servers: configuring SSL certificate on RDWeb IIS Web Site. To do so:

- Open a Windows session on each RDWA server and then launch the IIS manager console by running **InetMgr.exe** from the "**Run**" menu
- Expand up to "**Sites**", right-click on "**Default Web Site**" and select "**Edit Bindings...**":

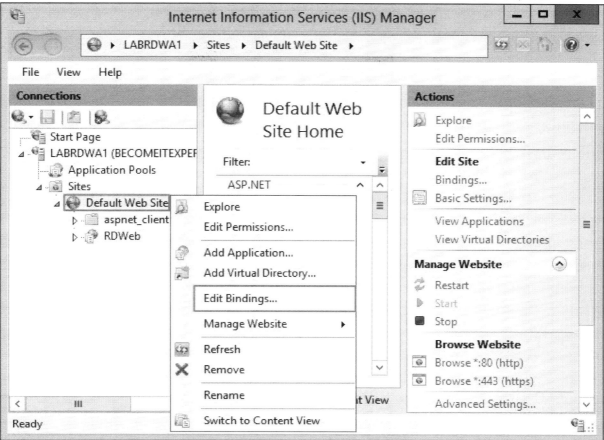

- Select "**https**" and click on "**Edit...**"
- Specify "**PortalApps.becomeitexpert.lan**" as a Host name and check that "PortalApps.BecomeITExpert.lan" SSL certificate is selected then click **OK**

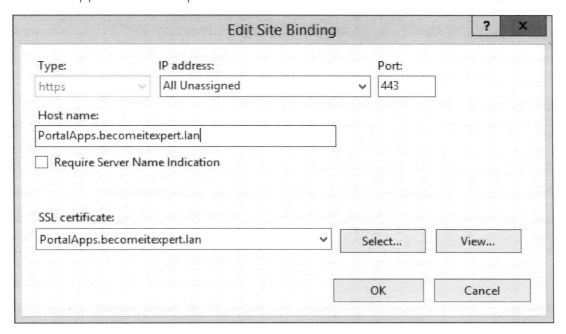

- Open the Command Prompt (cmd.exe) or Windows PowerShell as Administrator and type **IISReset /Restart** to restart the IIS service.
- Repeat the same actions on the second RDWA server "**LABRDWA2**".

 PortalApps.BecomeITExpert.lan SSL certificate must be imported into each client's computers that should connect to your RDWA Portal.

Configuring SSL certificate for RD Gateway

The same SSL certificate post-deployment task must be performed on all RDG servers. So open IIS Manager and edit the Bindings and then configure RDGateway.becomeitexpert.lan as a host name and select the appropriate SSL certificate:

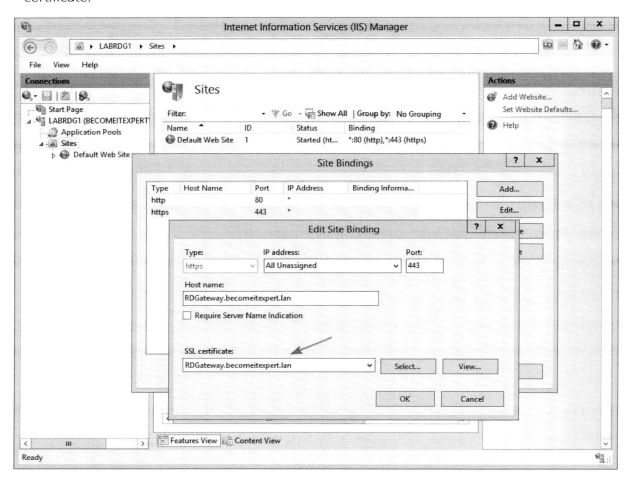

Now if you open the RDG Manager console on each RDG server, the following notification message will appear. You just have to click "**Yes**" to restart the RDG Gateway service so that the change (import of the new SSL certificate) will be taken into account.

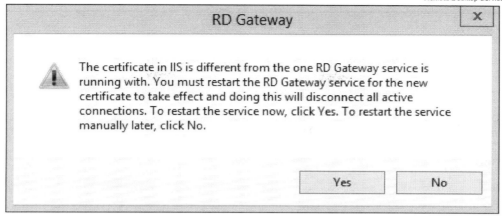

Finally, note that all the SSL certificates we created for each RD role service are considered as "Untrusted level". This is due to the SSL certificate type: "Self-signed". If you have your own PKI or sign your RDS SSL certificates by a valid CA, their security level become "Trusted" on the Deployment Properites dialog box.

 In a production environment, you must sign your SSL certificate by a valid CA to ensure a high security level.

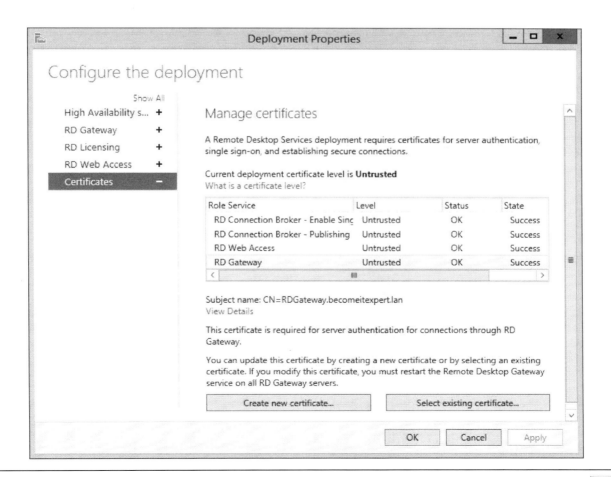

 All RDS self-signed SSL certificates we created can be imported automatically using a Group Policy Object.
- Computer Configuration | Windows Settings | Security Settings | strategies of public key | Trusted Root Certification Authorities

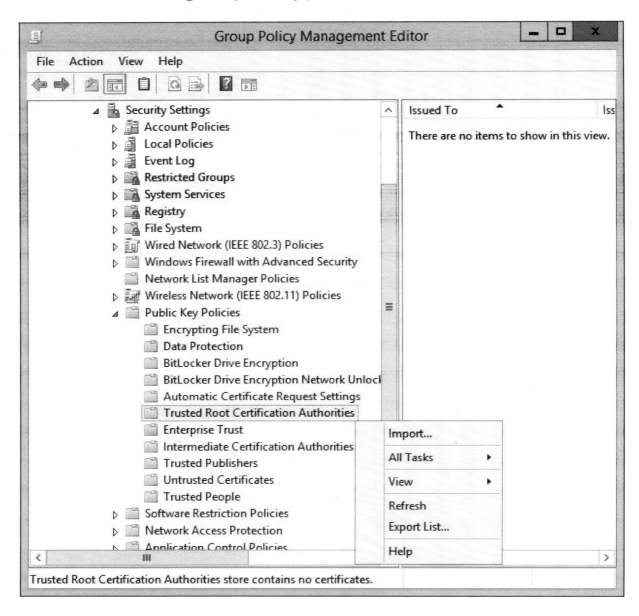

Just right-click on "**Trusted Root Certification Authorities**" and select "**Import...**" then follow the Wizard instructions to select and import all RDS certificates.
Finally, run **GPUpdate** from a DC to refresh a GPO engine.

To be sure that all SSL certificates were automatically imported into your network machines, open a Windows Session on LABW81 client computer and run MMC > Certificates > Compute Account > Local Computer > Certificates > Trusted Root Certification Authorities > Certificates. As shown below, all RD******.becomeitexpert.lan certificates are presents.

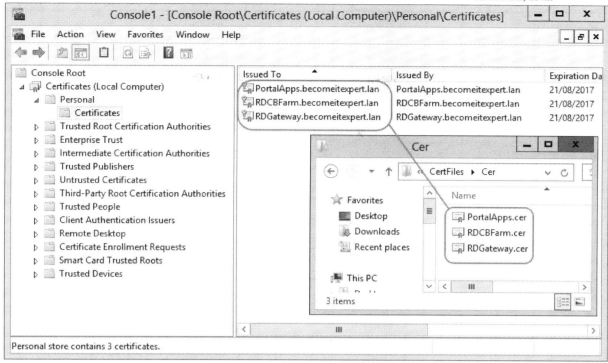

Test your deployment RDS 2012 R2 in Mode HA

Now that all RDS components are correctly configure, we will be able to make a final test of our RDS deployment.

RD Web Access

We will first test the RD Web Access portal (in HA mode). In order to do so:

- Open a Windows session on the client computer "**LABW81**"
- Open Internet Explorer and connect to :
    - https://PortalAppsBecomeITExpert.LAN/RDWeb
- If the RDWA role service SSL certificate (PortalApps.BecomeITExpert.lan) is correctly imported, the error message related to the SSL certificate disappears and IE bar address look like the image below :

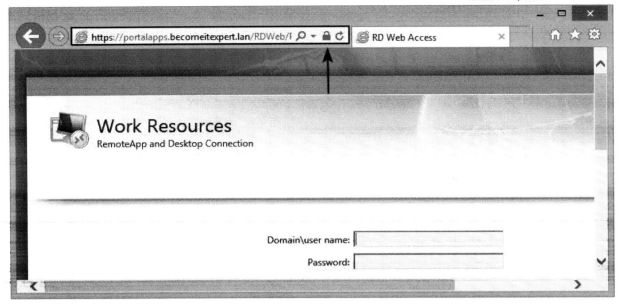

- Click on 🔒 icon to confirm that the connection between your client computer and the RD Web Access server(s) is encrypted:

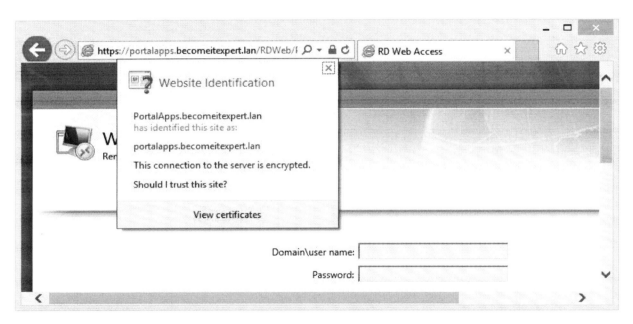

⇨ RD Connection Broker & Gateway

Now that we configured RDCB role service in HA mode, all remote clients will attempt RDCB Farm (RDCBFarm.BecomeITExpert.lan) before connecting to the RD resource (RemoteApp Program, Desktop...) hosted on the RDSH servers. The RDCB Farm is considered as a Host (as a Resource) with its IP address. So this resource must be added to the RAP policy on all RDG Gateway. To do so :

- Open a Windows session on each RDG Server and luanch the RD Gateway Manager console
- Expand the root node (RDG server name) > Policies > Resource Authorization Policies, select the RDG_**RAP_RDSUsers** and then select "**Properites**"

- Under "**Network Resource**", click the "**Browse...**" button and then create a new Resource group (**RDSResources**) to which you add the following three resources (hosts) : LABRDSH1, LABRDSH2 and RDCBFarm

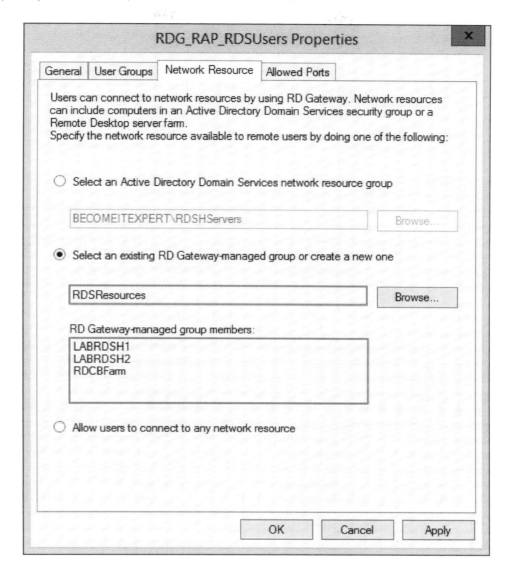

- From LABW81 client, open IE and connect to the RDWA Portal using your credentials. Once authenticated, the following notification message is displayed: **Connected to RemoteApp and Desktop Connections**. This means that the RDCB SSO SSL certificate is taken into account and you are automatically connected to the Remote Desktop WorkSpace (Work Resource by default)

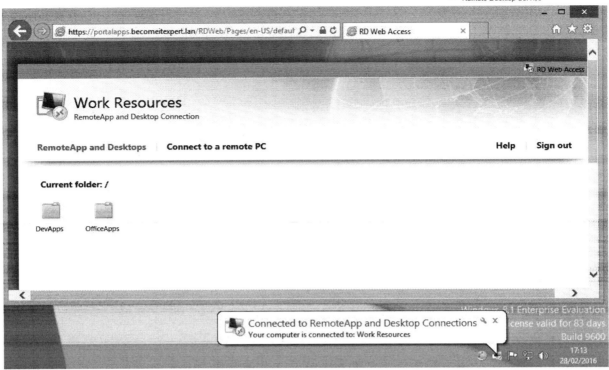

- Start a RemoteApp Program and note that you connect first to the RD Gateway farm (RDGateway.BecomeITExpert.lan) before connecting the RD Connection Broker farm (RDCBFarm.BecomeITExpert.lan) that redirect you to one of the two RDSH servers that host the RemoteApp Program you want to access

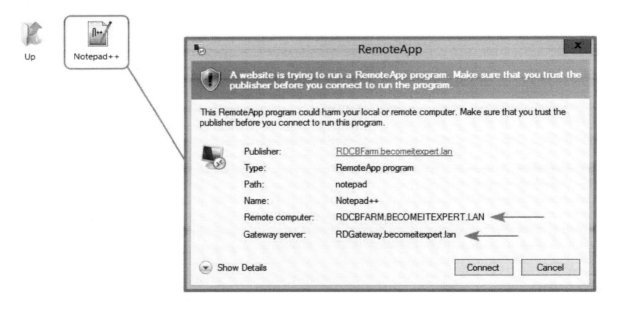

 If you have configured a "System Message", remote users will see it before connecting to the RemoteApp Program or Desktop.

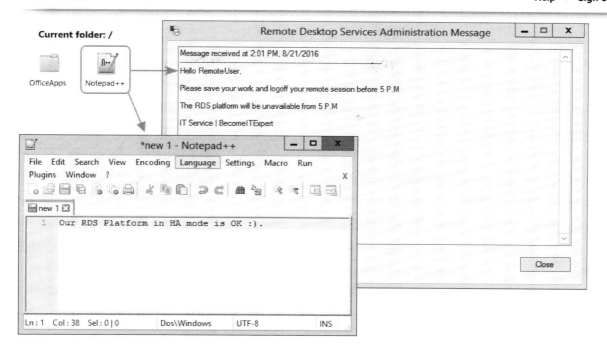

Chapter 12. Planning for preserving user state

In a session collection with multiple RD Session Host servers, the connections from clients are load balanced across the RD Session Host servers by the RD Connection Broker server. By default, when a user connects to a specific RD Session Host server, a local profile is created for that user on the RD Session Host server. The next time a user connects, the RD Connection Broker may direct the client to a different RD Session Host server, where a different local profile is created. Each time users sign in, they may be using a different profile on a different RD Session Host server. This means that user state information such as application configuration, Desktop configuration, Favorites, and Documents are not the same across sessions. To provide a consistent user experience, you should preserve user state across multiple RD Session Host servers.

If users have desktop computers and session-based virtual desktops, you also need to consider whether you want user state to be preserved between desktop computers and the virtual desktops. This can be complicated by the fact that session-based virtual desktops may not have the same configuration as the desktop computers, and, consequently, it may not make sense to synchronize all of the user state information. For example, synchronizing Desktops may result in desktop shortcuts appearing that point to applications that are not available on the RD Session Host servers.

Roaming Profiles

Roaming user profiles can be used to synchronize user state, but they synchronize entire user profiles. This typically is not desired for session-based desktops because not all user state information needs to be synchronized between desktop computers and RD Session Host servers. If you use roaming profiles for the desktop computers in your organization and you want to ensure that roaming profiles are not used on the RD Session Host servers, then you can configure the **msDSPrimaryComputer** attribute for users and enable the Download Roaming Profiles on Primary Computers Only Group Policy setting.

You also can set user properties for roaming user profiles that are specific to RD Session Host servers, as shown in the figure below. If you configure the Profile Path, then a user connecting to a session based virtual desktop uses the specified profile path rather than a roaming profile configured on the Profile tab. Effectively, the RDS user profile becomes a roaming profile used only when connected to an RD Session Host server.

Instead of configuring individual user accounts with RDS-specific profiles, you can use Group Policy. In a Group Policy object that applies to the RD Session Host servers, you can configure settings in:

Computer Configuration | Policies | Administrative Templates | Windows Components | Remote Desktop Services | Remote Desktop Session Host | Profiles

There are two relevant settings:

- **Set Path For Remote Desktop Services Roaming User Profile**: specify a UNC path for storing all user profiles. A subfolder for each user is created automatically.
- **Use Mandatory Profiles on the RD Session Host Server**: indicates that the path specified in the Set Path for Remote Desktop Services Roaming User Profile setting contains a mandatory profile that can't be modified. When this setting is enabled, the UNC path for profiles does not contain subfolders for each user.

Folder redirection

Folder redirection also is an option for users with session-based virtual desktops. You can redirect only the folders that are suitable for use on the virtual desktops and desktop computers. Commonly redirected folders include Documents, Favorites, and AppData\Roaming.

If you use folder redirection for desktop computers and don't want folder redirection used when users sign in to the RD Session Host servers, you can use the **msDS-PrimaryComputer** attribute in user accounts just as you can for roaming profiles. In addition to configuring the attribute, you need to enable the Redirect Folders on Primary Computers Only Group Policy setting.

User Profile Disks (UPD)

RDS in Windows Server 2012 and 2012 R2 offers the option to configure user profile disks to preserve user state across sessions. A User Profile Disk is a VHDX file that is mounted to the user's profile path at C:\Users\%username% on the RD Session Host. The user profile disk is mounted during sign in.

During a user's session, all changes to the profile write in his or her VHDX file, and when the user signs out, his or her profile disk is unmounted. The administrator specifies the maximum size of user profile disks and can limit which folders in a user profile are included in or excluded from a user profile disk.

User profile disks are configured individually for each session collection and can't be shared among collections. A share is specified in the collection configuration to store the user profile disks. All RD Session Host servers in the collection have access to the user profile disks in the share. This provides users with consistent user state from any RD Session Host server in the collection.

User profile disks can be used in conjunction with folder redirection and roaming user profiles. Folder redirection will reduce the size of user profile disks and allow the redirected folders to be accessed from desktop computers. Roaming user profiles are synchronized with the user profile disk. From a server management perspective, one benefit of user profile disks is controlling the amount of data stored on the C drive of RD Session Host servers. Large user profiles stored on RD Session Host servers can cause the C drive to run low on space and cause performance issues. Because user profile disks are stored on a network share and mounted in C:\Users, the C drive never is used to store profile data.

The primary consideration when planning user profile disks is ensuring that the necessary disk space is available for network storage. To ensure that network storage is sufficient, you need to determine the average user profile size. The amount of storage that you need to allocate for user profile disks is the average user profile size times the number of users plus an allowance for growth in both the number of users and the average profile size.

User profile disks are dynamically expanding VHDX files. By default, the maximum size of a user profile disk is 20 GB, but you can set this to be larger or smaller depending on the needs of your users.

When you configure the share for user profile disks, all RD Session Host servers need to have "**Full Control**" permissions. This allows the RD Session Host servers to create and manage the user profile disks. When you configure a collection with user profile disks, these permissions are assigned automatically.

Enable User Profile Disks

Follow the instructions below to enable and configure User Profile Disks on "MyApps" Collection:

- Open a Windows session on the DC "**LABDC1**"
- Create a new Share (on C:\) with the following informations:
    - Folder name   : UPD_RDUsers
    - Share name   : UPD_RDUsers
    - Share Permissions   : **Everyone = Read**

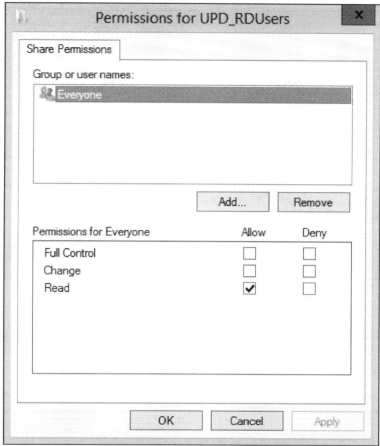

- Open RDMS console and Select "MyApps" Collection
- Under "**TASKS**", select "**Edit Properties**"
- Click on "**User Profile Disks**" and then tick "**Enable user profile disks**" option
- Specify \\LABDC1\UPD_RDUsers as a location. As shown in the image below, we will limit the maximum size of a user profile disk to 5 GB:

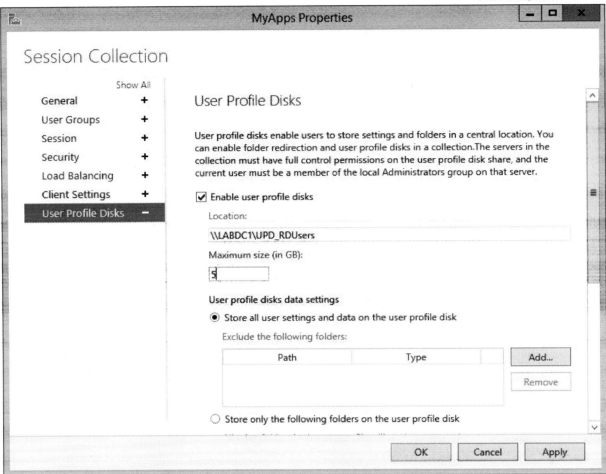

- Click "**OK**" to close the Wizard.

Once the UPD configured, the following actions are performed:

- A new VHDx "Template" is automatically created and placed on the specified Share (\\LABDC1\UPD_RDUsers in our case): **UVHD-template.vhdx**
- "**Full Control**" permissions are automatically configured on the share for all RD Session Host servers that are part of the Collection on which UPD was enabled.

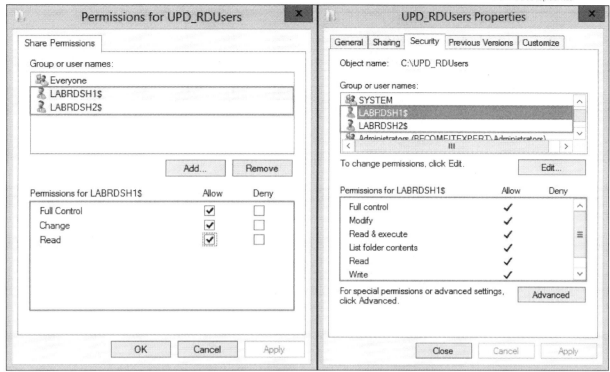

> If other RD Session Host servers are added to a Collection with UPD enabled, Full Control permissions are automatically configured for these servers on the Share that hosts UVHD files.

Now open a Remote Desktop Session or launch a RemoteApp program that is published on the "MyApps" Collection and then check the availability of your user profile disk generated in the shared folder \\LABDC1\UPD_RDUsers.

As shown below, the VHDx file name syntax is "UVHD-ADUserAccount's_SID"

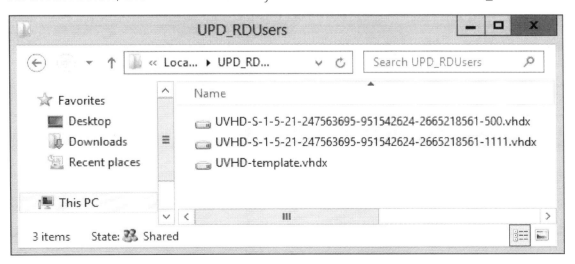

Once created, VHDx disk can be mounted from the Windows Explorer, it may be useful for you if you want to access to a specific RD user profile to check, remove, or move their Data.

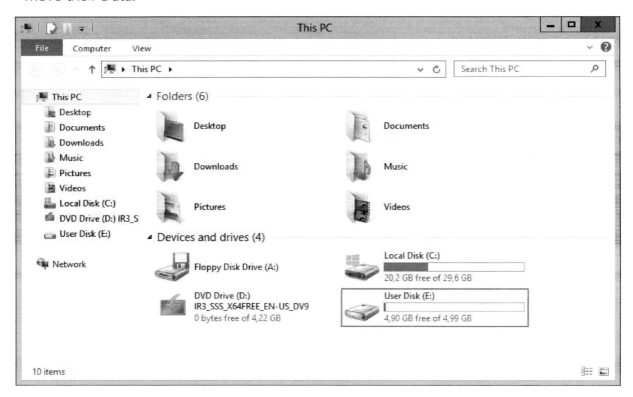

Chapter 13. Configuring RDS Universal Printing

Printing a document from a RD Session Host server sounds simple, just press the 'Print' button. But depending on the complexity of your environment, it can easily turn into a complicated affair.

Applications are usually executed on a system sans local printers with network printers in a different subnet, which often employ firewalls and routers. In order to print, a user must have the printer installed on their local machine and the administrator must have the print driver already set up on the RDSH server(s).

Multiply this innumerable times over and you face an out of control printing situation in a RDS environment that is near impossible to handle. The combinations of users, printers, and print drivers make this task overwhelming to say the least, not to mention expensive and time consuming.

Microsoft's Solution: Easy Print

Microsoft formulated a printing software solution called Microsoft Easy Print, which uses universal driver technology in order to combat these issues.

Microsoft EasyPrint is a native feature in Windows Server 2008, 2008 R2 and 2012 R2.

Easy Print is a Microsoft solution for limiting the amount of drivers used by printers that are mapped via the client printer redirection option.

How Easy Print works?

With Client Printer Redirection the printers available to the client are mapped into the RDS session. The redirected printer needs to be connected to a printer driver that is available on the RDS server. Before Easy Print, you needed to have the same printer driver available on the RDS server as this one was available on the connected client. This could lead to having hundreds of printer drivers on one server, which was not optimal for stability of the RDS server.

A kind of solution was to "map" a specific client driver to a driver which was available on the server. For several similar printers this worked pretty well, but for many printers the exact driver was needed.

Easy Print solves this issue by mapping the Client Printer to the Easy Print driver instead. So you don't need to have a separate driver for the printers that are connected via the Client Printer Redirection.

The figure below shows how Easy Print work:

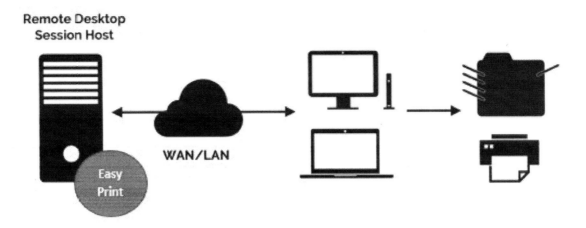

Configuring Easy Print

The Easy Printer feature is enabled by default when RDS is installed. The whole configuration is done via RDMS console or Group Policy Objects.

- Configuration via RDMS: **Collection Properties > Client Settings > Printers**

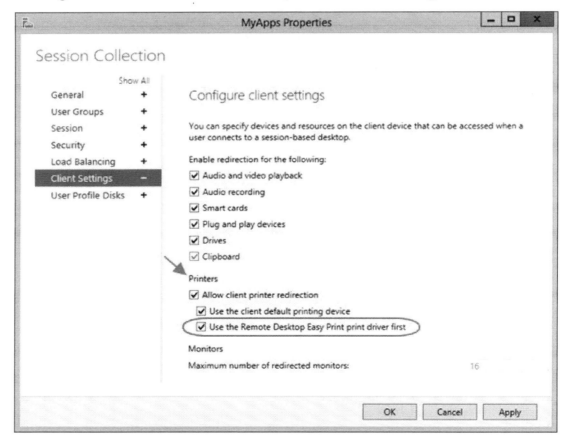

- Configuration via Group Policy Objects:

The configuration settings can be found at: Computer Configuration | Policies | Administrative Templates | Windows Components | Remote Desktop Services | Remote Desktop Session Host | Printer Redirection

- o Parameter:
  - Use Remote Desktop Easy Print printer drive first

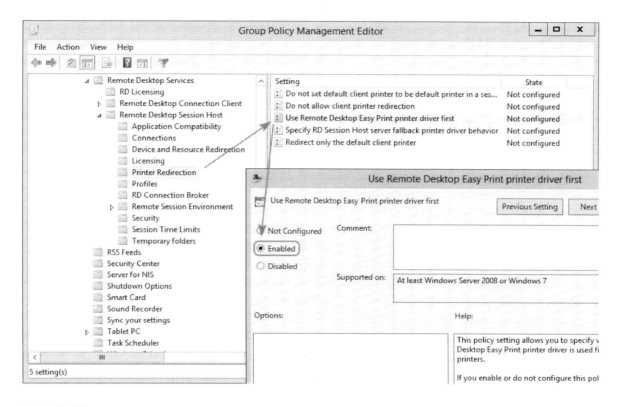

 Easy Print feature requires RDP 6.1 or higher

Chapter 14. Configure your RDS 2012 R2 infrastructure using GPO

Group Policy Objects (GPO) can be used to configure and manage most RDS role services and components, including:

- RD Clients settings
- Device and Resource Redirection
- Security
- RD Licensing
- RD Gateway
- Session Time Limits
- Remote Session Environment
- RD Connection Broker
- ...

There are more than 100 Group Policy settings provided with Windows Server 2012 R2 and dedicated for Remote Desktop Services role.

These Group Policy settings are organized by the Group Policy nodes in which they are located in the Group Policy Management Console (GPMC):

Computer Configuration Group Policy Settings

All Group Policy settings are available under:

Computer Configuration / *Policies* / *Administrative Templates* / *Windows Components* / *Remote Desktop Services*

User Configuration Group Policy Settings

All Group Policy settings are available under:

User Configuration / *Policies* / *Administrative Templates* / *Windows Components* / *Remote Desktop Services*

Under Computer Configuration, Group Policy settings are spread over three folders:

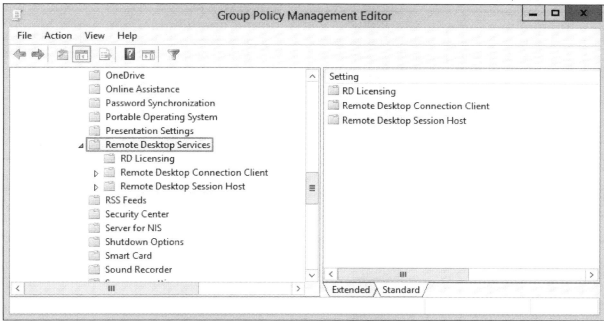

Remote Desktop Session Host folder contains all RDS settings available from the "RDS Deployment Properties" and "Session Collection Properties":

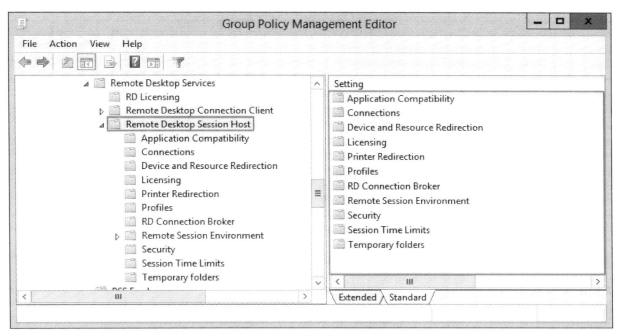

In the following example, we will configure the Printer Redirection options to redirect only the default client printer to the Remote Desktop Session, in order to do this:

- Open a Windows session on the DC "**LABDC1**"
- Type **GPMC.MSC** from the "**Run**" Menu and then click "**OK**"
- Navigate to the OU (Organizational Unit) that contains your RDSH Servers computers accounts and create a new GPO (*RDS_Config*). As shown below, our RDSH servers computers accounts are stored in "**RDS2012R2\Servers**" OU:

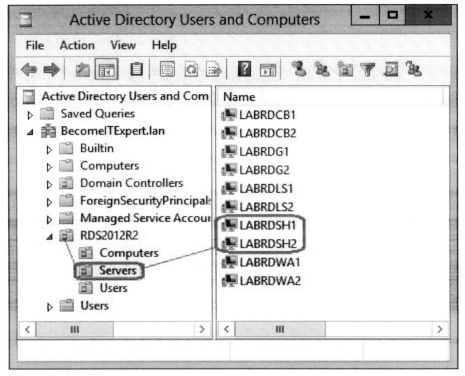

- Right-click on the OU and select "**Create a GPO in this domain, and Link it here...**":

- Once created, right-click on the new GPO and select "**Edit...**"
- Navigate to: **Computer Configuration** | Policies | Administrative Templates | Windows Components | Remote Desktop Services | Remote Desktop Session Host | Printer Redirection
- Double-click on the setting "**Redirect only the default client printer**"
- Select "**Enabled**" to activate the parameter and then click "**OK**" to validate:

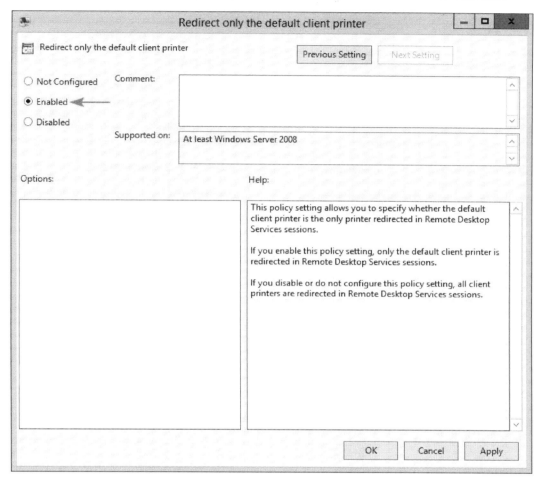

- Open the Command Prompt (cmd.exe) or Windows PowerShell and type the following command to refresh the Group Policy engine : **GPUpdate**

You can also enable or disable other Device and Resource Redirection, as shown below, under "Device and Resource Redirection", you can Allow (or not) audio recording redirection, COM port redirection, Drive redirection...:

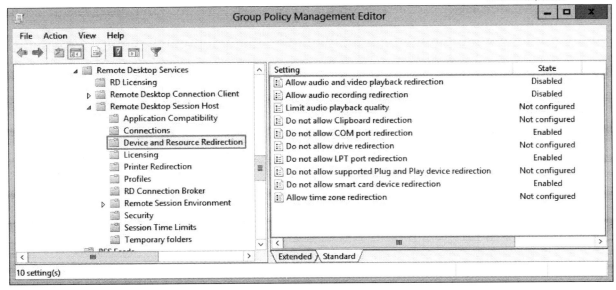

Finally, note that once configured via GPO, all RDS parameters available from RDMS console cannot be modified, indeed, configuration made via GPO has priority against the RDMS or any other RDS GUI tool:

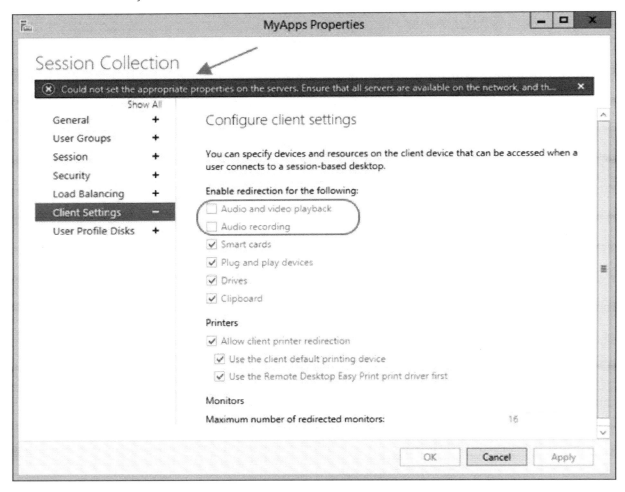

Chapter 15. Customize your RD Web Access Portal

Once deployed, the RD Web Access portal looks like the image below:

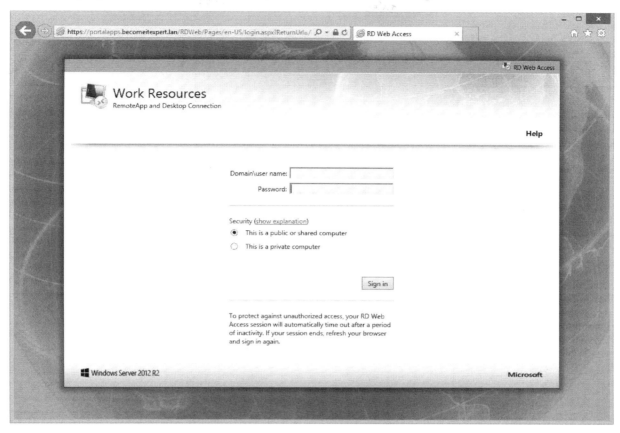

You may need to customize your RD Web Access Portal, to make for example, the following changes:

- Replace the default RDP logo by your company logo /customer logo
- Change the default WorkSpace name "Work Resources" with a more suitable name
- Change the default description "RemoteApps and Desktop Connection" with a more suitable description
- Change the default background image

This section describes all instructions you need to follow to customize your RDWA Portal.

Change the default Workspace name

By default, the Workspace name is "**Work Resources**", this information can only be changed via Windows PowerShell using the "**Set-RDWorkSpace**" Cmd-Let.

The current Workspace name can be viewed using the "**Get-RDWorkSpace**" Cmdlet.

Use the following command to display the current workspace name:

Get-RDWorkSpace –ConnectionBroker LABRDCB1.BecomeITExpert.lan

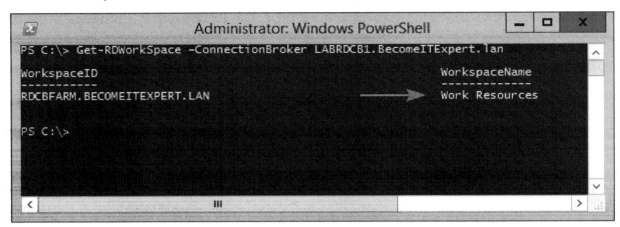

In the following example, "BecomeITExpert Apps Store" will be defined as the Workspace name of our RDS deployment, so the following command is used:

Set-RDWorkSpace -name "BecomeITExpert Apps Store"
-ConnectionBroker LABRDCB1.BecomeITExpert.LAN

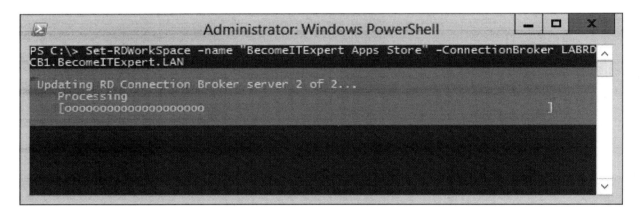

 As explained earlier in this book, after configuring the RDCB role service in HA mode, only one RDCB server is set as an "Active RDCB server". The current Active RDCB server of our deployment is LABRDCB1, it's for this reason that it was used with –ConnectionBroker parameter.

Change the default Workspace description

Follow the instructions below to change the default Workspace description:

- Open a Windows session on each RDWA server
- Open Windows Explorer and navigate to the following location:

- o C:\Windows\Web\RDWeb\Pages\en-US\
- Right-click on "**RDWAStrings**" file and then select "**Edit**"
- Locate the default Workspace description: **RemoteApp and Desktop Connection** and then replace this default text by your text.
- In the following example, the description below will be used:
Welcome to BecomeITExpert RemoteApps and Desktop Web Store.

 The same change must be made on all RDWA servers of the deployment. In our case, you have to modify the RDWAStrings file on both LABRDWA1 and LABRDWA2.

Change the default images used by the RD Web Access Portal

All the images used by the RDWA portal are stored in the following subfolder: C:\Windows\Web\RDWeb\Pages\Images

You may replace any image with an image of your own. For example:

- Replacing **logo_02.png** changes the image in the upper left hand corner of the pages

- Replacing **logo_01.png** changes the image in the upper right hand corner of the pages

- Changing **bg_globe_01.jpg** changes the big globe background image of the whole site
- Changing **banner_01.jpg** changes the main page banner where the company main logo and the default words "Work Resources" are located.

There are two ways replace images:

- Backup and then overwrite an image in the Images folder with one of your own with the same name as the original
- Drop a new image into the Images folder and then change the text in Site.xsl page to reflect the new image name.

 Make sure the resolution is at least as large and the height and width ratio match the image you are replacing

Adding the Password Reset feature to RD Web Access

Follow the instructions below to enable the RD Web Access Password reset option for your remote users:

- Open a Windows session on each RDWA server
- Open the "**Run**" Menu and launch **InetMgr.exe** tool
- Expand and navigate to: [ServerName] | Sites | Default Web Site | RDWeb | Pages
- Double-click on "**Application Settings**" and then on "**PasswordChangeEnabled**"
- Replace the default value (false) by "**true**" and click "**OK**"

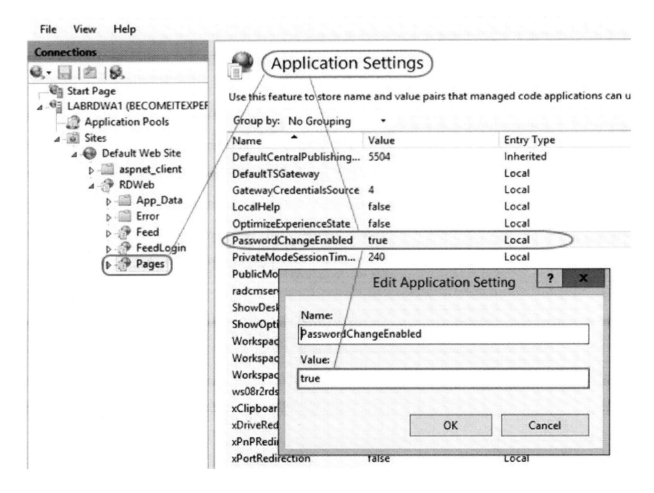

- Now, open Windows Explorer and navigate to the following location:
  C:\Windows\Web\RDWeb\Pages\en-US
- Edit the "**login.aspx**" file and locate the word "**UserPass**"
- Copy & Paste the following code, as shown in the image below:

```
<tr>
<td align="right">
<a href="password.aspx" target="_blank">Change your password</a>
</td>
</TR>
```

- Save the changes and close the login.aspx file

After changing some of the options listed above, the RD Web Access look like the image below:

When remote users click on « **Change your password** » option, the following web page is opened:

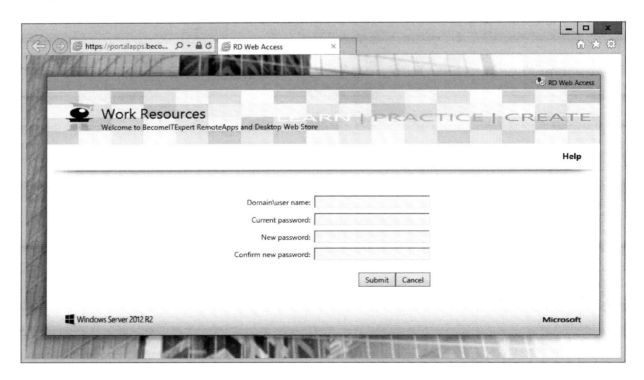

Chapter 16. Troubleshoot your RDS 2012 R2 infrastructure

Diagnostic Tools you need to know

Windows Diagnostic Tools

As discussed earlier in this book, Remote Desktop Management Server (RDMS), replaces all snap-ins available with RDS Windows Server 2008 and 2008 R2 and provides centralized management of the Remote Desktop infrastructure.

RDMS also includes several tools that allow you to troubleshoot issues related to your RDS 2012 R2 infrastructure:

- **SERVICES**: allows you to manage all RDS Windows Services and view their Status/Start Type
- **PERFORMANCE**: allows you to configure "Performance Alerts" related to all RDS infrastructure components /roles services.
- **BPA** (**B**est **P**ractices **A**nalyzer): allows you to reduce best practice violations by scanning RDS role services and reporting them to you.
- **EVENTS**: allows you to view all events logs related to the RDS infrastructure components.

These tools are available from **RDMS** console, under "**Servers**" pane.

In addition, the "**RD Licensing Diagnoser tool**" that's installed by default with the RDSH server provides useful informations to help you identifying RDS licensing issues.

 It's recommended to run RDS Best Practices Analyzer (BPA) at least once a month to check the health state of the RDS Infrastructure and its components.

BPA tool can be run from the "**Servers**" pane, under "**BEST PRACTICES ANALYZER**".

Click on "**TASKS**" and select "**Start BPA Scan**", the following dialog box appears, select the server(s) you want to scan and then click on "**Start Scan**":

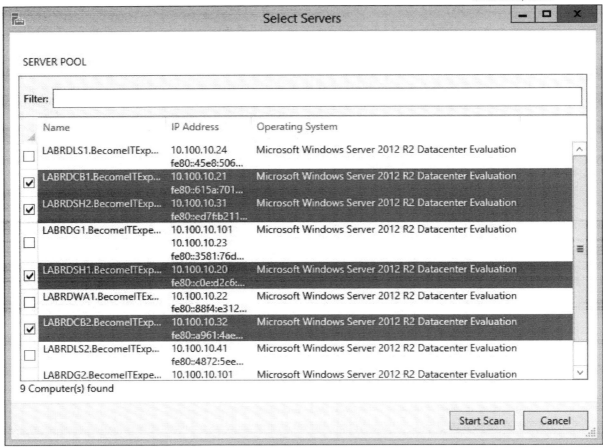

Depending on the number of RD servers that are evaluated, the BPA scan can require a few minutes to finish. Once the scan is finished, all collected informations are displayed under "BEST PRACTICES ANALYZER"

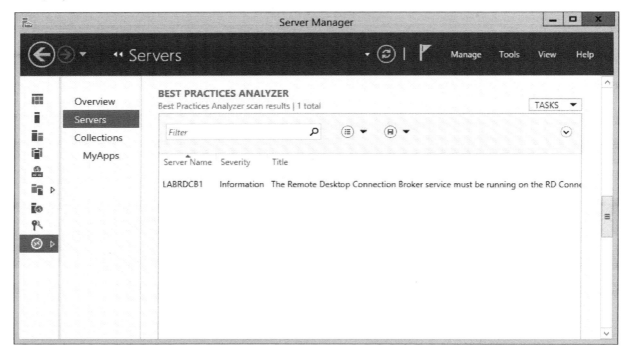

RDS Diagnostic Tool

Remote Desktop Services Diagnostic Tool is a free tool designed to help troubleshoot and diagnose issues with RDS deployments. The RDS Diagnostic Tool can be used to get the current status of an RDS deployment or diagnose various types of issues in the deployment. The tool has several tabs that display different aspects of the deployment.

You can download the tool from the Microsoft Download Center at:

http://www.microsoft.com/en-us/download/details.aspx?id=40890

Note that there are some prerequisites for running the tool:

- The tool needs to be run under a user account with Administrator privileges.
- The tool needs to be launched on the RD Connection Broker server.
- The tool supports only Windows Server 2012 and Windows Server 2012 R2 deployments (no support for Windows Server 2008 and 2008 R2).

RDS Diagnostic Tool

Windows services used by RDS

The Remote Desktop Services 2012 R2 infrastructure requires the following Windows Service to work correctly:

Display Name	Service Name
Remote Desktop Services *(formerly 'Terminal Services service')*	TermService
Remote Desktop Configuration	SessionEnv
Remote Desktop Services UserMode Port Redirector	UmRdpService

If the "**TermService**" Windows service is stopped, no Remote Desktop Connection will be accepted /allowed.

The service "**SessionEnv**" allows you to make changes on the RDS deployment: Collection Creation, Edit the Collection /RemoteApp properties, adding new RD server to the Deployment. It's also responsible for session maintenance activities that require SYSTEM context. These include per-session temporary folders, RD themes, and RD certificates.

"**UmRdpService**" Windows Service allows the redirection of Printers, Drives and Ports for Remote Desktop connections.

Try to stop these services to note the risks and impacts made on your RDS infrastructure.

Note that other Windows sub-services related to the RDS infrastructure exist, refer to the table below:

RDS Role service	Windows Service
Host service of the session (RDSH)	TermService
Service Broker (BDR)	Tssdis
The Gateway Service RDS (RDG)	TSGateway
The License Service RDS (RDLS)	TermServLicensing
Service Web Access (RDWA)	No Windows service associated with this component

From "**Remote Desktop Services**" pane, under "**Servers**", select one or more RD servers and then scroll down until "**SERVICES**" section, all Windows services related to the selected Remote Desktop Servers are listed:

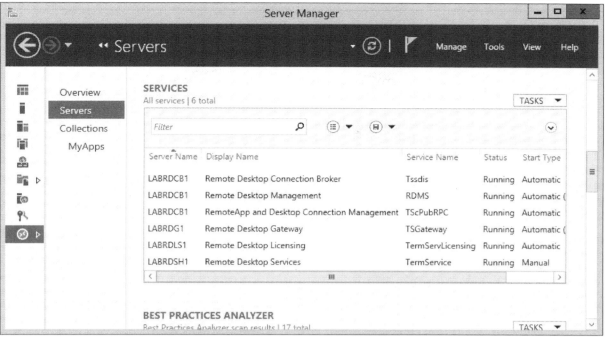

About the author

Hicham KADIRI is a 3-time Microsoft **MVP** (**M**ost **V**aluable **P**rofessional) in the Cloud and Datacenter Management Technologies category.

He is an infrastructure architect who specializes in system, virtualization and cloud technologies including : Windows Server /Server Core - Active Directory - Group Policy Objects - Hyper-V - WSUS - RDS /TSE /APP-V /MED-V /UE-V - Command /VBS /PowerShell scripting - SCCM/SCOM - MS Azure /Office365 /AWS - ADFS - IT Security (AppLocker /Cryptolocker /SRP /OS Hardening)

He has worked in a variety of technical roles for over 10 years and achieved several industry Certifications including Microsoft Certified Professional /IT Professional /System Administrator, Engineer and Specialist and also VMware Certified Professional-Datacenter Virtualization.

Hicham KADIRI is currently working as a Senior Infrastructure Architect at a multinational Company where he's in charge of design, implementation, migration and management of large Microsoft infrastructures.

He is also a Blogger (**https://hichamkadiri.wordpress.com**) and a Microsoft Technical French Contributor on Microsoft TechNet (Forum /Wiki /Gallery)